Soups and Stews

Marshall Cavendish London & New York

Edited by Isabel Moore

Published by
Marshall Cavendish Publications Limited
58 Old Compton Street
London W1V 5PA

© Marshall Cavendish Limited 1973, 1974, 1975, 1976

This material was first published by
Marshall Cavendish Limited
in the partwork *Supercook*.

This volume first published 1976

Printed by Henri Proost, Turnhout, Belgium

ISBN 0 85685 163 9

Contents

Key to symbols

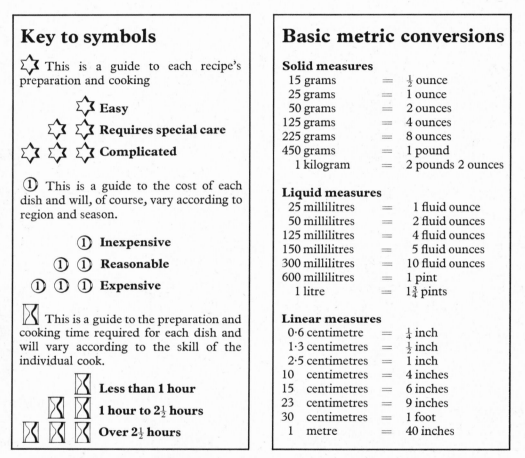

☆ This is a guide to each recipe's preparation and cooking

    ☆ **Easy**

   ☆ ☆ **Requires special care**

  ☆ ☆ ☆ **Complicated**

① This is a guide to the cost of each dish and will, of course, vary according to region and season.

    ① **Inexpensive**

   ① ① **Reasonable**

  ① ① ① **Expensive**

⧖ This is a guide to the preparation and cooking time required for each dish and will vary according to the skill of the individual cook.

    ⧖ **Less than 1 hour**

   ⧖ ⧖ **1 hour to $2\frac{1}{2}$ hours**

  ⧖ ⧖ ⧖ **Over $2\frac{1}{2}$ hours**

Basic metric conversions

Solid measures

15 grams	=	$\frac{1}{2}$ ounce
25 grams	=	1 ounce
50 grams	=	2 ounces
125 grams	=	4 ounces
225 grams	=	8 ounces
450 grams	=	1 pound
1 kilogram	=	2 pounds 2 ounces

Liquid measures

25 millilitres	=	1 fluid ounce
50 millilitres	=	2 fluid ounces
125 millilitres	=	4 fluid ounces
150 millilitres	=	5 fluid ounces
300 millilitres	=	10 fluid ounces
600 millilitres	=	1 pint
1 litre	=	$1\frac{3}{4}$ pints

Linear measures

0·6 centimetre	=	$\frac{1}{4}$ inch
1·3 centimetres	=	$\frac{1}{2}$ inch
2·5 centimetres	=	1 inch
10 centimetres	=	4 inches
15 centimetres	=	6 inches
23 centimetres	=	9 inches
30 centimetres	=	1 foot
1 metre	=	40 inches

American equivalents of food and measurements are shown in brackets.

Soups and stews for the family

Soups and Stews are basic to all cuisines and have been concocted, cooked — and enjoyed — almost since Man first discovered fire. They are flexible dishes, too, that actually taste even better a day or two after they're cooked (although we won't actually guarantee that these delicious recipes will last that long!).

With practically the whole world to choose from, it has been difficult to decide what to include in this book but, in the end, the compromise was made between the tried and true (such old favourites as Onion Soup, pictured below, recipe on page 6, Tomato Soup on page 9 and Lancashire Hot Pot on page 19) and the new-and-unfamiliar-but-delicious (see page 8 for our unusual recipe for Revythia, a Greek chick-pea soup and page 22 for the exotic Near Eastern Pork with Peanuts and Grapes).

All of these attractive dishes are sustaining enough to satisfy the most demanding family and economical enough not to shatter the family budget. But, of course, there are those special occasions (birthdays, anniversaries and so on) when you'll want to spend a bit more money on the food, a bit more time in the kitchen and, recognizing this, we have provided some specially selected recipes **For Special Occasions.** And this collection of slightly extravagant but superb dishes, all fit to grace the most elegant table, are absolutely guaranteed to make your party 'go' right from the start.

But perhaps the ultimate virtues of these recipes are that they're FUN to cook, and easy too. They take the monotony out of daily cooking and enable a busy mum to sit down with the family and actually enjoy the meal she has just prepared. And any recipes that do that make good cooking — and good eating — automatic!

1

Bean and Bacon Soup

☆ ① ⊠ ⊠ ⊠

This filling and tasty soup may be served at an informal lunch or dinner. It also makes a good main course, served with crusty French bread, for a family lunch or supper.

6 SERVINGS
- 12 oz. [1½ cups] dried butter [lima] beans
- 2 lb. bacon hock with bone
- 1 large onion, cut in quarters
- 1 large garlic clove, crushed
- 3½ pints [8¾ cups] water
  bouquet garni, consisting of 4 parsley sprigs, 1 thyme spray, and 1 bay leaf tied together
- ½ teaspoon white pepper
- 20 large black olives, cut in half and stoned
- 3 tablespoons chopped parsley

Delicious and nutritious, Bean and Bacon Soup is a perfect family meal.

Put the beans in a bowl and cover with water. Leave them to soak overnight.

Drain the beans and put them in a large saucepan with the bacon, onion and garlic. Cover with the water, place the pan on high heat and bring to the boil.

Add the bouquet garni and pepper to the pan and stir well. Lower the heat and simmer the soup for 1½ to 2 hours, or until the beans and bacon are cooked and tender.

Remove the bacon hock and cut the meat into pieces. Remove the bouquet garni and discard. Purée some of the beans, using a fork or an electric blender and add to the soup to thicken it. Stir in the bacon pieces and olives. Taste and add salt and more pepper, if necessary.

Pour the soup into individual bowls, sprinkle with the parsley and serve hot.

Carrot Soup

☆ ① ⊠

Good quality, young carrots are necessary to provide a clear fresh colour and flavour for this soup. Carrot Soup may be served plain, or with croûtons of bread, fried diced potatoes, or a spoonful of boiled rice.

4 SERVINGS
- 1½ oz. [3 tablespoons] butter
- 1 lb. carrots, scraped and coarsely grated
- 8 oz. potatoes, peeled and roughly diced
- 1 medium-sized onion, finely chopped
- 1½ pints [3¾ cups] chicken stock or water

½ teaspoon salt
½ teaspoon freshly ground white
pepper
2 tablespoons double [heavy] cream

In a medium-sized saucepan, melt the butter over moderate heat. Reduce the heat to low and add the carrots, potatoes and onion. Cook for 15 minutes, stirring occasionally with a wooden spoon to prevent the vegetables from sticking to the pan. Add the stock or water, salt and pepper and simmer for another 20 minutes, or until the vegetables are quite soft.

Remove the pan from the heat. Pour the contents of the pan through a strainer placed over a medium-sized mixing bowl. With a wooden spoon press the vegetables through the strainer, or put them through a blender.

Return the soup to the saucepan and reheat it. If the soup is too thin, simmer, uncovered, until the soup thickens. Stir in the cream, taste and add more salt and pepper if necessary. Serve immediately, in hot bowls.

Colourful Cock-a-Leekie is a soup invented by the Scots that's absolutely guaranteed to sustain the family on cold winter days!

Cock-a-Leekie

☆ ① ⋈ ⋈ ⋈

A warming, traditional Scots soup of chicken and leeks, Cock-a-Leekie is served with hot crusty bread. It may be served as a filling first course to a dinner, or as a light but sustaining lunch or supper for the whole family.

6 SERVINGS

1 x 4 lb. chicken
4 pints [5 pints] water
7 leeks, including 2 inches of the green stems, thoroughly washed, trimmed and cut into ½-inch long slices
2 celery stalks, trimmed and coarsely chopped into ½-inch lengths
2 oz. [⅓ cup] pearl barley
bouquet garni, consisting of 4 parsley sprigs, 1 thyme spray, 1 bay leaf and 6 peppercorns tied together in a piece of cheesecloth
1 teaspoon salt
½ teaspoon freshly ground black pepper
1 tablespoon finely chopped fresh parsley

Place the chicken in a large saucepan and pour over the water. The chicken should be covered with water so add more if necessary. Place the pan over moderately high heat and bring the water to the boil. With a metal spoon, carefully skim off any scum that rises to the surface of the liquid.

Add the leeks, celery, barley, bouquet garni, salt and pepper and reduce the heat to very low.

Partly cover the pan with the lid on a slant and simmer the chicken for 1½ to 2 hours, or until the meat is almost falling off the bones.

Remove the pan from the heat and transfer the chicken to a wooden board or platter. Leave it to cool slightly. With a metal spoon, skim the fat off the surface of the cooking liquid. Remove and discard the bouquet garni.

With a small, sharp knife, carefully detach the chicken meat from the skin and bones. Discard the skin and bones. With your hands, shred the chicken coarsely and return it to the cooking liquid in the saucepan.

Place the pan over moderate heat and simmer the soup for 5 minutes to reheat it thoroughly.

Remove the pan from the heat and pour the soup into a warmed soup tureen or individual warmed soup bowls. Sprinkle the parsley over the soup and serve at once.

Cream of Chicken Soup

☆ ☆　　① ①　　◰ ◰

This is a simple, but nevertheless delicious, Cream of Chicken Soup. To add colour, it may be sprinkled with chopped parsley.

6 SERVINGS

2 lb. chicken backs and wings
2½ pints [6¼ cups] water
2 celery stalks, trimmed
1 bay leaf
1 small onion studded with 2 cloves
1 teaspoon salt
10 peppercorns
8 fl. oz. single cream [1 cup light cream]
8 fl. oz. [1 cup] milk
1½ oz. [3 tablespoons] butter blended with 1½ oz. [⅓ cup] flour

Place the chicken pieces in a large saucepan and cover them with the water. Add the celery, bay leaf, onion, salt and peppercorns. Place the pan over high heat and bring to the boil.

Reduce the heat to low, cover the pan and simmer for 2 hours.

Remove the pan from the heat and strain the liquid into a bowl. Pick out the chicken pieces, detach the meat from the bones and set the meat aside. Discard the skin, bones, vegetables and flavourings.

Return the strained liquid to the saucepan and stir in the cream and milk. Place the pan over moderate heat and bring the soup to the boil.

Roll the butter mixture into small pieces and add them, one by one, to the soup, stirring continuously.

Add the meat to the soup and bring to the boil again. Serve at once.

Cucumber and Pork Soup

☆　　　①　　　◰

A simple yet exotic Chinese soup with a fresh flavour, Cucumber and Pork Soup makes an interesting and different first course for a family meal.

6 SERVINGS

2¼ pints [5⅝ cups] chicken stock
1 teaspoon salt
1 tablespoon soy sauce
8 oz. pork fillets, cut into very thin strips
2 medium-sized cucumbers, peeled, halved lengthways, seeded, and cut into ¼-inch slices

In a large, heavy saucepan, combine the chicken stock, salt and soy sauce together. Add the strips of pork to the pan and bring the mixture to the boil over moderate heat. Cook for 10 minutes.

Add the cucumbers to the pan and

Exotic Cucumber and Pork Soup.

bring the soup back to the boil. Boil for 3 minutes, or until the cucumbers are translucent. Pour the soup into a warmed tureen and serve at once.

Georgian Vegetable Soup

☆　　　①　　　◰

An inexpensive and easy-to-make soup, Georgian Vegetable Soup may be served with crusty bread and butter for a light and warming winter lunch or dinner.

4-6 SERVINGS

1 oz. [2 tablespoons] butter
1 large onion, thinly sliced and pushed out into rings
2 tablespoons flour
2 pints [5 cups] chicken stock
1 lb. tomatoes, blanched, peeled, seeded and coarsely chopped
1 lb. leeks, washed, trimmed and cut into ½-inch lengths
1 teaspoon salt
½ teaspoon black pepper
½ teaspoon dried oregano
1 bay leaf
1 tablespoon chopped fresh chives

In a large saucepan, melt the butter over moderate heat. When the foam subsides, add the onion and cook, stirring occasionally, for 5 to 7 minutes, or until it is soft and translucent but not brown. Remove the pan from the heat and, with a wooden spoon, stir in the flour to make a smooth paste.

Gradually stir in the chicken stock. Add the tomatoes, leeks, salt, pepper, oregano and the bay leaf to the pan.

Return the pan to high heat and bring the soup to the boil, stirring constantly. Reduce the heat to low, cover the pan and simmer for 20 minutes or until the leeks are soft.

Remove the pan from the heat. Remove and discard the bay leaf. Pour the soup into a warmed soup tureen, sprinkle on the chives and serve immediately.

Knuckle of Lamb and Tomato Soup

☆ ① ⊠ ⊠ ⊠

Serve this substantial main dish soup with plenty of crusty bread.

4 SERVINGS

3 lamb's knuckles, each sawn into 2 pieces
4 peppercorns
1½ teaspoons salt
  large bouquet garni, consisting of 8 parsley sprigs, 2 thyme sprays and 2 bay leaves tied together
1 onion, halved
1 oz. [2 tablespoons] butter
1 onion, finely chopped
1 garlic clove, chopped
1 tablespoon flour
2 lb. canned peeled tomatoes, drained and coarsely chopped
1 teaspoon dried basil
¼ teaspoon pepper

Put the knuckles, peppercorns, 1 teaspoon salt, the bouquet garni and the halved onion in a large saucepan. Pour in enough water just to cover the knuckles.

Place the pan over high heat and bring the water to the boil. Reduce the heat to low, cover the pan and simmer for 1 hour.

Remove the pan from the heat and lift out the knuckles. Strain the liquid into a mixing bowl and set aside.

With a sharp knife, remove the meat from the knuckle bones and cut it into 1-inch pieces. Set the meat aside.

When the cooking liquid is cold, skim the fat off the surface with a metal spoon. Reserve 5 fluid ounces [⅝ cup].

In a medium-sized saucepan, melt the butter over moderate heat. When the foam subsides, add the chopped onion and garlic and fry, stirring occasionally, for 5 to 7 minutes, or until the onion is soft and translucent but not brown.

With a wooden spoon, stir in the flour. Cook, stirring constantly, for 2 minutes.

Remove the pan from the heat and stir in the reserved cooking liquid. Return the pan to the heat and add the tomatoes, basil, the remaining salt and the pepper. Bring the mixture to the boil, stirring.

Reduce the heat to low and add the knuckle meat. Simmer gently for 10 minutes, or until the meat is reheated.

Remove the pan from the heat and serve at once.

Mushroom Soup

☆ ① ① ⊠

This easy-to-make Mushroom Soup, flavoured with oregano and cayenne pepper, tastes delicious served with croûtons.

4-6 SERVINGS

1 oz. [2 tablespoons] butter
1 small onion, finely chopped
3 tablespoons flour
1 teaspoon salt
½ teaspoon black pepper
¼ teaspoon dried oregano
⅛ teaspoon cayenne pepper
1½ pints [3¾ cups] chicken stock
1 lb. mushrooms, stalks removed, wiped clean and sliced
1 bay leaf
5 fl. oz. double cream [⅝ cup heavy cream]

In a large saucepan, melt the butter over moderate heat. When the foam subsides, add the onion and fry, stirring occasionally, for 5 to 7 minutes, or until the onion is soft and translucent but not brown.

Remove the pan from the heat. With a wooden spoon, stir in the flour, salt, pepper, oregano and cayenne to make a smooth paste. Gradually stir in the stock, being careful to avoid lumps. Stir in the mushrooms and bay leaf.

Return the pan to the heat and bring the soup to the boil, stirring constantly. Reduce the heat to low, cover the pan and simmer for 30 minutes.

Uncover the pan and stir in the cream. Cook the soup, stirring constantly, for 2 to 3 minutes or until it is hot.

Remove the pan from the heat. Remove and discard the bay leaf and serve.

Mushroom Soup is easy to make.

Onion Soup

Onion Soup (pictured on page 1) *may be served for lunch with croûtons and chopped spring onions* [scallions], *chives or water-cress.*

4 SERVINGS

1 tablespoon butter
2 tablespoons vegetable oil
1 garlic clove, crushed
1 small potato, peeled and chopped
8 medium-sized onions, peeled
1 pint [2½ cups] milk
1 pint [2½ cups] water
½ teaspoon salt
½ teaspoon freshly ground black pepper
¼ teaspoon dried sage
¼ teaspoon dried thyme
1 tablespoon cornflour [cornstarch] dissolved in 3 tablespoons water
4 fl. oz. single cream [½ cup light cream]

In a medium-sized frying-pan, melt the butter with the oil over low heat. When the foam subsides, add the garlic and cook, stirring occasionally, for 4 minutes. Increase the heat to moderately high. Add the potato and cook, stirring frequently, for 4 minutes or until it is brown.

Meanwhile, thinly slice two of the onions and push the slices out into rings.

Using a slotted spoon, remove the potato from the pan and drain it on kitchen paper towels.

Add the onion rings to the frying-pan and cook them, stirring occasionally, for 5 to 7 minutes or until they are soft and translucent but not brown. Remove the pan from the heat. Using the slotted spoon, remove the onion rings from the pan and place them to drain on kitchen paper towels. Set aside.

Place the remaining onions on a chopping board and, using a sharp knife, chop them finely.

Pour the milk and water into a large saucepan. Add the salt, pepper, sage, thyme, potato and chopped onions. Place the pan over low heat and bring the liquid to the boil. Cover the pan and simmer for 30 minutes or until the onions are tender.

Remove the pan from the heat. Strain the onion mixture into a large mixing bowl. Using the back of a wooden spoon, press down on the vegetables in the strainer to extract all the juices. Discard the contents of the strainer.

Rinse out the saucepan and wipe it dry. Return the strained soup to the saucepan. Add the reserved onion rings and stir in the cornflour [cornstarch] mixture. Place the pan over moderate heat and, stirring constantly, bring the soup to the boil.

Simmer for 1 minute, stirring constantly.

Remove the pan from the heat. Stir in the cream and pour the soup into warmed individual soup bowls.

Serve immediately.

Pea Soup with Ham

A warming winter soup, Pea Soup with Ham may be served on its own or with French bread for a sustaining lunch or supper. For the best results, make the soup the day before you intend to serve it and reheat.

4-6 SERVINGS

1 ham hock, soaked overnight and drained
5 pints [6¼ pints] water
bouquet garni, consisting of 4 parsley sprigs, 1 thyme spray and 1 bay leaf tied together
1 teaspoon freshly ground black pepper
1 oz. [2 tablespoons] butter
1 medium-sized onion, thinly sliced
1 medium-sized garlic clove, crushed
2 small carrots, scraped and thinly sliced
8 oz. [1 cup] split peas, soaked overnight and drained

Place the ham hock in a large saucepan and pour over 4 pints [5 pints] of the water. Add the bouquet garni and black pepper. Place the pan over moderate heat and bring the water to the boil, skimming off any scum that rises to the surface. Reduce the heat to low, cover the pan and simmer for 1½ to 2 hours or until the meat is very tender and nearly falling off the bone.

Remove the pan from the heat. Using tongs or two large spoons, transfer the ham hock to a plate. Cover it with aluminium foil. Set aside.

Strain the cooking liquid into a large mixing bowl and set aside to cool to room temperature. Then place the bowl in the refrigerator and chill for 2 hours or until a layer of fat has formed on the top of the liquid. Remove and discard the layer of fat. Set the cooking liquid aside.

In a large saucepan, melt the butter over moderate heat. When the foam subsides, add the onion, garlic and carrots and fry, stirring occasionally, for 5 to 7 minutes or until the onion is soft and translucent but not brown.

Add the split peas to the pan and cook, stirring constantly, for 5 minutes.

Add the cooking liquid and the remaining water and bring it to the boil over high

Thick and warming, Pea Soup with Ham is full of goodness for family meals, yet elegant enough to serve as a first course to a special dinner party.

heat, stirring occasionally. Cover the pan, reduce the heat to low and simmer for 2 hours or until the peas are tender. Remove the pan from the heat and set aside to cool for 15 minutes. Then purée the mixture in a food mill or electric blender. Return the puréed soup to the pan. Add more water if the soup is too thick for your taste. Set aside.

Cut the meat from the ham hock bone, discarding any fat. Using a sharp knife, chop the meat into very small pieces.

Add the meat to the pan and return the pan to low heat. Simmer the soup for a

further 10 minutes or until the meat is heated through and the soup is hot but not boiling.

Remove the pan from the heat and transfer the soup to a warmed tureen or individual warmed soup bowls. Serve immediately.

Potato Soup

☆   ①   ⊠

A warm soup, easy-to-make and inexpensive, Potato Soup makes a tasty lunch for the whole family. Serve with lots of brown bread and butter.

4-6 SERVINGS

2 oz. [¼ cup] butter
2 tablespoons vegetable oil
1 medium-sized onion, finely chopped

3 medium-sized leeks, white parts only, trimmed and very thinly sliced
6 potatoes, peeled and finely chopped
1 teaspoon salt
½ teaspoon freshly ground black pepper
1 pint [2½ cups] home-made chicken stock
10 fl. oz. [1¼ cups] milk

In a medium-sized saucepan, melt the butter with the oil over moderate heat. When the foam subsides, add the onion and cook, stirring occasionally, for 5 to 7 minutes or until the onion is soft and translucent but not brown. Add the leeks and potatoes and cook, stirring and turning occasionally, for 10 to 12 minutes or until the potatoes are lightly and evenly

browned. Season with the salt and pepper and pour over the chicken stock and milk. Increase the heat to high and bring the liquid to the boil, stirring constantly. Reduce the heat to moderately low, cover the saucepan and simmer the liquid for 25 minutes.

Remove the pan from the heat and pour the soup through a fine wire strainer held over a large mixing bowl. Using the back of a wooden spoon, rub the vegetables through the strainer. Discard the pulp left in the strainer.

Return the soup to the saucepan and place the pan over moderately low heat. Cook the soup, stirring occasionally, for 5 minutes.

Remove the pan from the heat. Pour the soup into a large warmed soup tureen or individual soup bowls and serve immediately.

Quebec Vegetable Soup

This soup originates from Canada, although soups bearing similar names and having similar ingredients are found throughout the world. It is a rich and simple-to-make soup.

4 SERVINGS

1 oz. [2 tablespoons] butter
2 tablespoons flour
2 pints [5 cups] chicken stock
1 carrot, scraped and chopped
1 celery stalk, trimmed and chopped
1 teaspoon salt
½ teaspoon black pepper
¼ teaspoon grated nutmeg
4 egg yolks
8 fl. oz. double cream [1 cup heavy cream]

In a large, heavy saucepan, melt the butter over moderate heat. When the foam subsides, remove the pan from the heat and stir in the flour to make a smooth paste. Gradually stir in the stock, being careful to avoid lumps. Stir in the carrot, celery, salt, pepper and nutmeg.

Return the pan to the heat and bring the soup to the boil, stirring constantly.

Reduce the heat to low, cover the pan and simmer the soup for 30 to 35 minutes or until the vegetables are very tender.

In a small mixing bowl, beat the egg yolks and the cream together with a fork until they are thoroughly combined.

Stir the cream and egg yolk mixture into the soup and cook, stirring constantly, for 4 to 5 minutes or until the soup is thick and smooth. Do not let the soup boil or it will curdle.

Remove the pan from the heat. Pour the soup into a warmed soup tureen or individual soup bowls and serve.

Revythia

GREEK CHICK-PEA SOUP

A filling soup from Greece made with chick-peas, Revythia will be a warming, nourishing dish for the family during even the coldest weather.

3-4 SERVINGS

2 pints [5 cups] chicken stock
12 oz. [2 cups] dried chick-peas, soaked overnight and drained
2 fl. oz. [¼ cup] olive oil
bouquet garni, consisting of 4 parsley sprigs, 1 thyme spray

and 1 bay leaf tied together
1 teaspoon salt
1 teaspoon freshly ground black pepper
1 teaspoon lemon juice
2 medium-sized onions, chopped
1 tablespoon chopped fresh parsley

In a large, heavy-based saucepan, bring the stock and the chick-peas to the boil over high heat, skimming off any scum which rises to the surface with a metal spoon.

Reduce the heat to low and add the olive oil, bouquet garni, salt, pepper and lemon juice. Cover the pan and simmer for 1 hour. Add the onions and continue simmering the soup for a further ½ hour, or until the chick-peas are very tender.

Remove the pan from the heat. Using a slotted spoon, remove about half the chick-pea mixture and either rub it through a strainer, using the back of a wooden spoon, or purée the mixture in a blender. Return the puréed chick-pea mixture to the pan. Return the pan to the heat and bring the soup to the boil over

Delicate but sustaining Quebec Vegetable Soup.

This satisfying Tomato Soup is a traditional British favourite.

moderate heat, stirring constantly. Taste the soup and, if necessary, add more salt and pepper.

Remove the pan from the heat and pour the soup into a warmed soup tureen. Sprinkle over the parsley and serve immediately.

Thrifty Soup

A filling and, as its name suggests, economical soup, Thrifty Soup may be served as a light lunch or supper.

8 SERVINGS

2 oz. [¼ cup] pearl barley
1½ lb. pork shoulder, excess fat removed, boned and cut into 1-inch cubes
3 pints [7½ cups] cold water
large bouquet garni consisting of 8 parsley sprigs, 2 thyme sprays and 2 bay leaves, tied together
1½ teaspoons salt
1 teaspoon white pepper
3 carrots, scraped and diced
1 large leek, trimmed, cleaned and chopped

3 celery stalks, trimmed, cleaned and chopped
6 potatoes, peeled and thinly sliced
1 pint [2½ cups] milk
1 tablespoon chopped fresh parsley

Place the pearl barley, pork, water, bouquet garni, salt and pepper in a large saucepan and bring the mixture to the boil over high heat. Reduce the heat to low, cover the pan and cook for 1½ hours, stirring occasionally.

Add the carrots, leek, celery and potatoes, increase the heat to high and bring the liquid to the boil, stirring constantly. Reduce the heat to moderate, cover the pan and cook for a further 15 to 20 minutes or until the vegetables are very tender. Stir in the milk and continue cooking for 4 to 5 minutes or until the liquid is hot.

Remove and discard the bouquet garni. Pour the soup into a warmed soup tureen and sprinkle over the parsley. Serve immediately.

Tomato Soup

This Tomato Soup allows the fresh taste of the tomatoes to predominate. For the family serve the soup with fresh bread or toasted rounds of French bread.

4 SERVINGS

1 oz. [2 tablespoons] butter
1½ lb. tomatoes, quartered
1½ pints [3¾ cups] chicken stock
1 medium-sized onion, finely chopped
1 bay leaf
½ teaspoon black pepper
¼ teaspoon salt
thinly pared rind of ¼ orange
2 teaspoons lemon juice
1 teaspoon sugar

In a medium-sized saucepan, melt the butter over low heat. When the foam subsides, add the tomatoes and cook for 10 minutes, stirring frequently. Increase the heat to moderate and add the stock, onion, bay leaf, pepper, salt and orange rind. When the liquid comes to the boil, reduce the heat to low, cover the pan and simmer for 45 minutes.

Remove the pan from the heat and pour the contents through a strainer into a medium-sized saucepan. Using the back of a wooden spoon, rub the tomato mixture through the strainer until only a dry pulp is left. Discard the pulp.

Add the lemon juice and sugar to the pan and place it over low heat. Bring the soup to the boil, stirring frequently. Remove the pan from the heat and pour the soup into a warmed soup tureen. Serve immediately.

Turkish Yogurt, Chicken and Barley Soup

This a refreshing and filling soup. Serve before a rather light main course.

4-6 SERVINGS

- 1 oz. [2 tablespoons] butter
- 2 medium-sized onions, finely chopped
- 2 pints [5 cups] home-made chicken stock
- 3 oz. [⅜ cup] pearl barley, soaked overnight and drained
- 1 tablespoon chopped fresh parsley
- 2 oz. cooked chicken, shredded
- ½ teaspoon salt
- ¼ teaspoon white pepper
- 1 pint [2½ cups] yogurt
- 1 tablespoon chopped fresh mint

In a large saucepan, melt the butter over moderate heat. When the foam subsides, add the onions and fry, stirring occasionally, for 5 to 7 minutes or until the onions are soft and translucent but not brown. Pour in the chicken stock, increase the heat to high and bring the liquid to the boil.

Reduce the heat to low and add the barley. Cover the pan and simmer for 30 minutes or until the barley is tender. Add the parsley, chicken, salt and pepper and simmer for 10 minutes. Remove the pan from the heat.

Pour the yogurt into a medium-sized mixing bowl. Using a fork, beat the yogurt until it is smooth. Pour in a little of the soup, beating constantly. Gradually pour the yogurt into the soup, beating all the time. Place the saucepan over moderate heat and heat the soup until it is very hot. Do not allow it to boil or it will curdle.

Stir the mint into the soup. Pour the soup into a warmed tureen and serve.

Vegetable Soup

One of the simplest and most economical soups, Vegetable Soup is warm and welcoming for the family on a cold day.

8 SERVINGS

- 2 oz. [¼ cup] vegetable fat
- 3 large carrots, scraped and diced
- 1 small swede [rutabaga], peeled and diced
- 2 large leeks, trimmed and coarsely chopped
- 2 large potatoes, peeled and diced
- 3 celery stalks, trimmed and coarsely chopped
- 6 tomatoes, blanched, peeled and coarsely chopped
- 4 oz. dried butter [lima] beans, soaked overnight and drained
- 1½ teaspoons salt
- 1 teaspoon freshly ground black pepper
- 3½ pints [8¾ cups] home-made beef stock
- 2 bay leaves
- 2 oz. frozen peas, thawed
- 1 tablespoon finely chopped fresh parsley

In a large, heavy-based saucepan, melt the vegetable fat over moderate heat. When the foam subsides, add the carrots, swede [rutabaga], leeks, potatoes and celery and cook, stirring occasionally, for 10 minutes.

Stir in the tomatoes, beans, salt and pepper and pour over the beef stock. Add the bay leaves, increase the heat to high and bring the mixture to the boil, stirring constantly.

Reduce the heat to moderately low, cover the pan and simmer, stirring occasionally, for 20 minutes or until the vegetables are soft.

Remove the pan from the heat and strain the soup through a large, fine wire strainer into a large mixing bowl. Remove and discard the bay leaves.

Remove about half the vegetables remaining in the strainer and add them to the strained stock in the bowl. With the back of a wooden spoon, rub the remaining vegetables through the strainer into a small mixing bowl. Alternatively, place the remaining half of the vegetables in the jar of an electric blender and blend at high speed for 30 seconds or until a purée is formed.

Transfer the purée to the saucepan and stir in the reserved stock and vegetable mixture. Place the saucepan over high heat, add the peas and bring the liquid back to the boil, stirring frequently. Reduce the heat to moderately low and simmer for a further 5 minutes or until the peas are tender.

Remove the pan from the heat and pour the soup into a warmed tureen or individual bowls. Sprinkle over the parsley and serve immediately.

Vegetable and Lentil Soup

A hearty and warming winter soup, Vegetable and Lentil Soup is almost a meal in itself served with crisp rolls and butter.

6 SERVINGS

- 1 lb. [2 cups] lentils, soaked overnight
- 4 pints [5 pints] cold water
- 1 ham bone or knuckle (optional)
- 8 oz. lean bacon, in one piece
- 1 leek, trimmed, cleaned and chopped
- 2 large carrots, scraped and chopped
- 1 medium-sized parsnip, peeled and chopped
- 2 celery stalks, trimmed and chopped
- 1½ teaspoons salt
- 2 tablespoons vegetable oil
- 2 medium-sized onions, finely chopped
- 2 tablespoons flour
- 1½ tablespoons cider vinegar
- 8 oz. garlic sausage, diced
- ¼ teaspoon dried thyme
- ½ teaspoon freshly ground black pepper

Drain the lentils in a colander and set aside.

In a large, heavy saucepan, bring the water to the boil over high heat. Remove the pan from the heat and add the lentils, ham bone or knuckle, if you are using it, bacon, leek, carrots, parsnip, celery and ½ teaspoon of the salt. Return the pan to moderate heat and bring to the boil. Reduce the heat to low and simmer the soup for 45 minutes.

Meanwhile, in a heavy frying-pan heat the oil over moderate heat. When the oil is hot, add the onions and cook, stirring occasionally, for 5 to 7 minutes, or until the onions are soft and translucent but not brown. Sprinkle the flour over the onions, reduce the heat to low and cook, stirring constantly, for 3 to 4 minutes or until the flour turns golden brown. Do not let the flour burn.

Remove the frying-pan from the heat and add about a cupful of the soup to the mixture, stirring well with a wooden spoon until the mixture is thick and creamy. Stir in the vinegar.

Pour the mixture in the frying-pan into the soup, stirring with a wooden spoon until the ingredients are well blended.

Cover the pan and simmer the soup over low heat for a further 1 hour, or until the lentils are tender. Add more water if the soup gets too thick.

Remove the ham bone or knuckle from the soup and discard it. Remove the bacon from the soup and cut it into small pieces.

Return the bacon pieces to the soup and add the sausage, thyme, the remaining salt and the pepper. Simmer for a further 4 to 5 minutes, or until the sausage is heated through.

Remove the pan from the heat and serve the soup at once.

Hearty Vegetable and Lentil Soup is adapted from a German recipe.

Yablonchni Apple Soup

☆ ① ① ✕ ✕ ✕

Yablonchni Apple Soup is a traditional Russian soup. It is delicious served ice cold with finely diced apple and croûtons fried in bacon fat.

4-6 SERVINGS

6 large cooking apples, peeled, cored and sliced
12 fl. oz. [1½ cups] water
1-inch strip pared lemon rind
2 tablespoons sugar
4 tablespoons blackcurrant jelly
26 fl. oz. [3¼ cups] (1 bottle) red wine
4 oz. [2 cups] fresh brown breadcrumbs

juice of 1 lemon
½ teaspoon ground cinnamon

Put the apples in a large saucepan and add the water, lemon rind and sugar. Place the pan over moderate heat and bring the liquid to the boil. Reduce the heat to low and simmer for 6 to 8 minutes or until the apples are tender. Remove and discard the lemon rind. Add the blackcurrant jelly, wine, breadcrumbs and lemon juice. Increase the heat to high and bring the mixture to the boil, stirring constantly. Add the cinnamon and remove the pan from the heat.

Pour the ingredients into a large fine strainer held over a large mixing bowl.

The Russians love rich fruit soups - hence Yablonchni Apple Soup with its fabulous blend of apples, blackcurrant jelly and red wine. Serve as first course to a special meal.

Using the back of a wooden spoon, rub the ingredients through the strainer until only a dry pulp is left. Discard the contents of the strainer. Set the purée aside to cool.

Place the bowl in the refrigerator and chill the soup overnight. Remove the bowl from the refrigerator and pour the soup into a soup tureen. Serve immediately.

Lamb and Lemon Soup

☆   ① ①   ✂ ✂

This thick, lemony lamb soup, flavoured with paprika and mint, is a traditional Turkish wedding soup. Ideally, it should be served with hot, flat Turkish bread.

6 SERVINGS

1 lb. boned leg of lamb, cut into
   1-inch cubes
2 oz. [½ cup] flour
3 tablespoons olive oil
2 pints [5 cups] water
2 medium-sized onions, quartered
2 medium-sized carrots, scraped
   and quartered
1 teaspoon salt
½ teaspoon black pepper
1 teaspoon cayenne pepper
3 egg yolks
2 tablespoons fresh lemon juice
2 oz. [¼ cup] butter, melted
2 teaspoons paprika
½ teaspoon ground cinnamon
2 tablespoons finely chopped fresh
   mint

Coat the lamb cubes with the flour, shaking off any excess.

In a large saucepan, heat the oil over moderate heat. Add the lamb cubes and cook them, stirring occasionally, for 4 to 5 minutes, or until they are lightly browned on all sides.

Pour the water into the pan and bring it to the boil.

With a metal spoon, skim any scum from the surface. Add the onions, carrots, salt, pepper and cayenne.

Reduce the heat to low, cover the pan and simmer for 1½ to 1¾ hours, or until the meat is very tender.

In a small mixing bowl, beat the egg yolks with a wire whisk. Beat in the lemon juice and 2 tablespoons of the hot lamb mixture in the saucepan.

Remove the pan from the heat and gradually beat in the egg yolk mixture. Return the pan to very low heat and, stirring constantly, warm the soup until it is hot. Do not allow it to boil or it will curdle.

Remove the pan from the heat and pour the soup into a warmed soup tureen.

In a small bowl, combine the melted butter, paprika and cinnamon. Spoon the mixture over the soup. Sprinkle on the mint and serve at once.

Windsor Soup

☆   ① ①   ✂ ✂

A traditional British recipe, Windsor Soup makes a sustaining first course. Serve with brown bread and butter.

8 SERVINGS

2 oz. [¼ cup] butter
8 oz. boned shin of beef, trimmed
   of fat and cubed
8 oz. lean boned leg of lamb,
   cubed
1 large onion, sliced
1 large carrot, scraped and sliced
2 oz. [½ cup] flour
4 pints [5 pints] home-made beef
   stock
   bouquet garni, consisting of 4
   parsley sprigs, 1 thyme spray
   and 1 bay leaf tied together
1 teaspoon salt
½ teaspoon cayenne pepper
4 fl. oz. [½ cup] Madeira

In a large saucepan, melt the butter over moderate heat. When the foam subsides, add the beef, lamb, onion and carrot and fry, stirring frequently, for 8 to 10 minutes or until the ingredients are lightly browned. Add the flour and cook for a further 5 minutes, stirring constantly.

Remove the pan from the heat. Gradually pour in the stock, stirring constantly and being careful to avoid lumps.

Lamb and Lemon Soup has the distinctively Middle Eastern flavour of lemon and mint, and is traditionally served at wedding feasts in Turkey.

Return the pan to the heat, increase the heat to high and bring the soup to the boil, stirring constantly. Reduce the heat to low and add the bouquet garni, salt and cayenne. Cover the pan and simmer the soup for 1½ hours or until the meat is very tender. Remove the pan from the heat.

Pour the soup through a fine strainer held over a large bowl and, using the back of a wooden spoon, rub the meat and vegetables through the strainer to form a purée. Alternatively, purée the meat and vegetables in an electric blender.

Return the soup to the saucepan and set the pan over moderate heat. Add the Madeira and cook the soup, stirring constantly, until it is very hot but not boiling. Remove the pan from the heat. Pour the soup into a warmed soup tureen or individual warmed soup bowls and serve at once.

Beef with Dumplings

☆ ① ⊠ ⊠ ⊠

This beef stew with mushrooms, dumplings and sour cream is a substantial and satisfying main dish. Serve it with a green vegetable or a fresh green salad and French bread.

4 SERVINGS

4 tablespoons flour
1 teaspoon salt
¼ teaspoon black pepper
2 lb. stewing steak, trimmed of fat and cut into 1-inch cubes
1 oz. [2 tablespoons] butter
1 tablespoon vegetable oil
1 large onion, finely diced
2 tablespoons brandy, warmed (optional)
1 bay leaf
2 pints [5 cups] home-made beef stock
6 oz. mushrooms, wiped clean
5 fl. oz. [⅝ cup] sour cream
DUMPLINGS
8 oz. breadcrumbs made from day-old white bread
4 tablespoons water
2 eggs, lightly beaten
¼ teaspoon salt
¼ teaspoon black pepper
1½ tablespoons chopped fresh parsley
1 onion, grated
½ teaspoon ground mace

Preheat the oven to warm 325°F (Gas Mark 3, 170°C).

Mix the flour, salt and pepper together on a large plate. Roll the beef cubes in the flour mixture until they are lightly coated.

In a large frying-pan heat the butter and oil over moderate heat. Add the onion and cook, stirring occasionally, for 5 to 7 minutes, or until it is soft and translucent. With a slotted spoon, remove the onion and set aside on a plate.

Add the beef cubes to the pan, a few at a time. Brown them well, adding more butter and oil if necessary. Remove the beef cubes as they brown and place them in a large ovenproof casserole.

If you are using the brandy, put it in a metal ladle. Set it alight and pour it, still burning, over the beef cubes in the casserole. When the brandy has stopped burning, add the onion to the casserole with the bay leaf and stock.

Cover the casserole and place in the oven to cook for 2 hours.

While the meat is cooking, make the dumplings. Put the breadcrumbs into a large mixing bowl. Add the water, a little at a time, and toss lightly with a fork. The breadcrumbs should be just moistened, not soggy. Still using the fork, lightly mix in the eggs. Add the salt, pepper, parsley, onion and mace.

With floured hands, shape the mixture into walnut-sized balls. Add the dumplings to the casserole, with the mushrooms, cover and cook for 30 minutes. Spoon over the sour cream just before serving.

Filling Beef with Dumplings needs only salad and lots of crusty bread to make a complete meal.

Beef Stew

This tasty Beef Stew may be served with boiled potatoes and braised carrots.

4 SERVINGS

2 lb. brisket of beef, trimmed of excess fat and cut into 1-inch cubes
3 tablespoons Dijon mustard
2 garlic cloves, crushed
2 tablespoons vegetable oil
2 lb. leeks, trimmed, washed and cut into 1-inch lengths
1 teaspoon sugar
2 tablespoons Worcestershire sauce
8 fl. oz. [1 cup] beef stock
8 oz. [2 cups] Gruyère cheese, finely grated

Preheat the oven to moderate 350°F (Gas Mark 4, 180°C).

Place the meat, mustard and garlic in a large mixing bowl and stir the ingredients together until the meat is coated with the mustard and garlic. In a large flameproof casserole, heat the oil over moderate heat. When the oil is hot, add the meat cubes and fry, stirring constantly, for 6 to 8 minutes or until the meat is lightly browned all over. Add the leeks, sugar and Worcestershire sauce.

Pour over the stock, increase the heat to high and bring the contents of the casserole to the boil. Remove the casserole from the heat and transfer it to the oven. Cook the meat, uncovered, for 2 hours, stirring occasionally.

Remove the casserole from the oven. Sprinkle over the cheese and return it to the oven. Cook for a further 10 to 15 minutes or until the cheese is bubbling and golden brown. Remove the casserole from the oven. Serve immediately, straight from the casserole.

Chilli Stew

Serve Chilli Stew with mashed potatoes or rice, bean salad and chilled lager.

4 SERVINGS

3 tablespoons vegetable oil
1 large onion, finely chopped
2 celery stalks, chopped
1 green pepper, white pith removed, seeded and chopped
2 garlic cloves, crushed
2 lb. minced [ground] beef
14 oz. canned peeled tomatoes, with the can juice reserved
5 oz. tomato purée

Beef Stew is an unusual blend of brisket, mustard and cheese.

1 teaspoon hot chilli powder
14 oz. canned kidney beans, drained
2 medium-sized cooking apples, cored and chopped
2 oz. prunes, stoned and chopped
2 tablespoons slivered almonds
4 oz. frozen French beans, thawed and chopped
$\frac{1}{4}$ teaspoon salt
$\frac{1}{2}$ teaspoon grated nutmeg

In a large, deep frying-pan, heat the oil over moderate heat. When the oil is hot, add the onion, celery, green pepper and garlic and fry, stirring occasionally, for 5 to 7 minutes or until the onion is soft and translucent but not brown. Stir in the minced [ground] beef and continue to fry, stirring frequently, for 5 minutes.

Add all of the remaining ingredients and stir well to mix. Bring the liquid to the boil. Reduce the heat to low, cover and simmer the mixture for 30 minutes. Uncover the pan and continue to simmer for a further 10 minutes.

Remove the pan from the heat and serve at once.

Flank Steak Stew with Herbs

☆   ①   ✕ ✕

A delicious and economical dish, Flank Steak Stew with Herbs makes a substantial dinner meal. Serve with green vegetables and a light, tossed salad.

6 SERVINGS

6 tablespoons seasoned flour, made with 6 tablespoons flour, 1 teaspoon salt and ½ teaspoon black pepper
3 lb. flank steak, cut into 1-inch cubes
3 oz. [⅜ cup] butter
2 tablespoons vegetable oil
3 medium-sized onions, thinly sliced
3 garlic cloves, crushed
1 large green pepper, white pith removed, seeded and chopped
2 oz. [¼ cup] walnuts, finely chopped
2 tablespoons finely chopped fresh parsley
½ teaspoon dried oregano
½ teaspoon dried thyme
2 bay leaves
1 teaspoon salt
16 fl. oz. [2 cups] home-made beef stock
2 tablespoons tomato purée
1 tablespoon cornflour [cornstarch] mixed to a paste with 2 tablespoons water

Place the seasoned flour on a large, shallow plate. Roll the meat cubes in the flour, shaking off any excess. Set them aside.

In a large flameproof casserole, melt 2 ounces [¼ cup] of the butter with the oil over moderate heat. When the foam sub-sides, add the meat cubes, a few at a time. Fry them, turning occasionally, for 5 minutes, or until they are lightly browned on all sides. With a slotted spoon, remove the meat from the pan and keep it warm while you fry the remaining cubes in the same way. Set the meat aside and keep it warm.

Add the remaining butter to the casserole and melt it over moderate heat. When the foam subsides, add the onions, garlic and green pepper. Cook, stirring occasionally, for 5 to 7 minutes, or until the onions are soft and translucent but not brown.

Stir in the walnuts, parsley, oregano, thyme, bay leaves and salt and cook the mixture, stirring occasionally, for 3 minutes. Pour in the beef stock and add the tomato purée. Stirring constantly, bring the liquid to the boil.

Return the meat cubes to the casserole. Reduce the heat to low, cover the casserole and simmer for 1½ hours, or until the meat is tender when pierced with the point of a sharp knife. Stir the stew from time to time during the cooking period.

Stir in the cornflour [cornstarch] mixture and simmer for 5 minutes, or until the sauce has thickened.

Remove the casserole from the heat and serve the stew at once, straight from the casserole.

Meat and Potato Hot Pot

☆ ① �X X X

An inexpensive satisfying dish, this Meat and Potato Hot Pot is simple to make. Serve with a mixed green salad and, to

These colourful Yiddish Meatballs taste even better than they look – AND they make an economical family lunch or supper, served with rice!

drink, some well chilled cider, lager or beer.

4-6 SERVINGS

2 oz. [¼ cup] butter
2 lb. potatoes, scrubbed and thinly sliced
2 medium-sized onions, thinly sliced
1 small swede [rutabaga], peeled and thinly sliced
1 lb. skirt or flank steak, cut into 1-inch pieces
2 teaspoons salt
½ teaspoon freshly ground black pepper
2 teaspoons chopped fresh thyme or 1 teaspoon dried thyme
1 tablespoon flour
1½ tablespoons Worcestershire sauce
10 fl. oz. [1¼ cups] water

Using ½ ounce [1 tablespoon] of the butter, grease a 5-pint [2-quart] hot pot or casserole.

Preheat the oven to warm 325°F (Gas Mark 3, 170°C).

Beginning and ending with the potatoes, layer the vegetables and the meat in the casserole. Sprinkle the layers with the salt, pepper, thyme, flour and Worcestershire sauce.

Pour in the water. Cut the remaining butter into small pieces and scatter them over the top layer of potatoes.

Cover the casserole and place it in the centre of the oven. Bake for 2½ to 3 hours, or until the vegetables and meat are tender when pierced with the point of a sharp knife.

Remove the casserole or hot pot from the oven and serve immediately, straight from the dish.

Yiddish Meatballs

☆ ① ① X X

An adaptation of a traditional Jewish recipe, Yiddish Meatballs are delicious meatballs in a sweet and sour tomato sauce. Serve with plain boiled rice and a mixed green salad and, to drink lots of chilled lager or dry white wine.

6 SERVINGS

2½ lb. lean beef, very finely minced [ground]
6 slices white bread, crusts removed, soaked in cold water and squeezed

2 medium-sized onions, finely grated
2 eggs, lightly beaten
2 teaspoons salt
1 teaspoon freshly ground black pepper
1 tablespoon Worcestershire sauce
2 tablespoons tomato ketchup
1 teaspoon grated nutmeg
3 fl. oz. [⅜ cup] vegetable oil or ground-nut oil

SAUCE
14 fl. oz. [1¾ cups] canned tomato juice
8 fl. oz. [1 cup] home-made beef stock
2 tablespoons tomato purée
1 teaspoon salt
½ teaspoon freshly ground black pepper
3 fl. oz. [⅜ cup] distilled malt vinegar
2 oz. [⅓ cup] soft brown sugar
1 tablespoon cornflour [cornstarch] mixed to a paste with 2 tablespoons water

In a large mixing bowl, combine the beef, bread, onions, eggs, salt, pepper, Worcestershire sauce, tomato ketchup and nutmeg. Using your hands, mix and knead the ingredients together for 5 minutes or until the meat mixture is thoroughly combined. Shape the meat mixture into 40 balls, approximately 1-inch in diameter. Set the meatballs aside.

In a large, flameproof casserole, heat the oil over moderate heat. When the oil is hot, add the meatballs, a few at a time, and fry, turning them frequently, for 6 to 8 minutes or until they are lightly browned all over. With a slotted spoon, remove the meatballs from the casserole as they brown and set them aside while you cook the remaining meatballs in the same way.

When all the meatballs have been cooked, add the tomato juice, beef stock, tomato purée, salt, pepper, vinegar, sugar and the cornflour [cornstarch] mixture to the casserole. Bring the mixture to the boil, stirring constantly.

When the sauce has thickened slightly, return the meatballs to the casserole. Reduce the heat to low, cover the casserole and simmer for 50 minutes to 1 hour or until the meatballs are cooked and very tender.

Remove the casserole from the heat. With a slotted spoon, remove the meatballs from the casserole and transfer them to a warmed serving dish. Taste the sauce and add salt and pepper if necessary. Pour the sauce over the meatballs and serve immediately.

Lamb

Lamb Ragoût

✡ ① ⧗ ⧗

A simple brown stew, Lamb Ragoût can be made early in the day and reheated immediately before serving.

4 SERVINGS

2 lb. shoulder of lamb, boned
3 tablespoons vegetable oil
2 tablespoons flour
1 teaspoon salt
½ teaspoon black pepper
1¼ pints [3⅛ cups] beef stock
2 small garlic cloves, crushed
  bouquet garni, consisting of 4
  parsley sprigs, 1 thyme spray
  and 1 bay leaf tied together
½ teaspoon dried thyme
8 small potatoes, peeled
12 small onions, peeled
12 small whole carrots, scraped
2 oz. [⅓ cup] raisins

Cut the lamb into 2-inch cubes and dry them well on kitchen paper towels. In a large, heavy saucepan, heat the oil over moderate heat. Add the meat, a few pieces at a time, and brown on all sides. As the cubes are done, transfer them to a dish and keep warm.

When all the pieces have been browned, return them to the pan and sprinkle with the flour, salt and pepper. Toss the pieces of meat with a spoon to coat them with the other ingredients. Cook over moderate heat, mixing occasionally, until the flour is lightly browned.

Add the stock, garlic, bouquet garni and thyme. Cover the pan and bring the stock to the boil. Reduce the heat to low and simmer for 40 minutes.

Add the potatoes, onions, carrots and raisins. Replace the lid and simmer for another 45 minutes or until the meat is tender when pierced with a sharp knife and the vegetables are cooked. Taste the stock and add more seasoning if necessary.

To serve, remove the bouquet garni and transfer the mixture to a warmed serving dish.

Lamb and Mushroom Stew

✡ ① ① ⧗ ⧗

A simple and nourishing dish, Lamb and Mushroom Stew makes a delicious family supper. Serve on a bed of rice.

4 SERVINGS

2 oz. [½ cup] seasoned flour, made
  with 2 oz. [½ cup] flour, 2
  teaspoons dried rosemary,
  1 teaspoon salt and ½ teaspoon
  black pepper
2 lb. boned leg of lamb, cut into
  1½-inch cubes

2 oz. [¼ cup] butter
3 medium-sized onions, thinly
  sliced
1 lb. mushrooms, wiped clean and
  sliced
½ teaspoon salt
¼ teaspoon black pepper
4 fl. oz. [½ cup] chicken stock
12 fl. oz. [1½ cups] sour cream

Place the seasoned flour on a shallow plate. Roll the meat cubes in it, shaking off any excess flour. Set the cubes aside.

In a large, deep frying-pan, melt the butter over moderate heat. When the foam subsides, add the onions and cook, stirring occasionally, for 5 to 7 minutes, or until they are soft and translucent but not brown. Add the lamb cubes and, stirring and turning occasionally, cook the mixture for 5 minutes, or until the meat is lightly and evenly browned.

Add the mushrooms, salt, pepper and chicken stock to the pan and mix well to blend. Bring the liquid to the boil. Reduce the heat to low, cover the pan and cook the mixture for 1 to 1¼ hours, or until the meat is very tender.

Stir in the sour cream and mix well to blend. Heat the mixture gently over low

Lamb Ragoût is a nutritious mixture of meat and vegetables.

heat until the sauce is hot but not boiling. Remove the pan from the heat and transfer the mixture to a warmed serving dish. Serve at once.

Lancashire Hot Pot

☆ ① ① ✕ ✕ ✕

Lancashire Hot Pot is a traditional British dish made with lamb chops, kidneys and oysters.

4 SERVINGS

1½ lb. potatoes, peeled and thickly sliced
1½ teaspoons salt
8 small lamb chops, trimmed of excess fat
4 oz. mushrooms, sliced
4 lambs' kidneys, cleaned, prepared and sliced
1 large onion, sliced
½ teaspoon black pepper
1 teaspoon dried thyme
12 oysters
10 fl. oz. [1¼ cups] beef stock

Preheat the oven to moderate 350°F (Gas Mark 4, 180°C).

Cover the bottom of a deep ovenproof casserole with a layer of half the potatoes. Sprinkle over ¼ teaspoon of salt. Arrange the chops on the potatoes and cover them with the mushrooms, kidneys and onion.

Sprinkle over 1 teaspoon of the salt, pepper and thyme. Cover with the oysters and the remaining potatoes. Pour in the stock and sprinkle the remaining salt over the potatoes.

Cover the casserole and place it in the oven. Cook for 2 hours. Remove the lid and increase the heat to fairly hot 400°F (Gas Mark 6, 200°C). Cook for a further 30 minutes, or until the potatoes are tender and golden brown.

Remove the casserole from the oven and serve at once.

Meatballs with Spicy Sauce

☆ ① ✕

This is a tasty dish, adapted from a North African recipe. Serve with boiled rice.

4 SERVINGS

2 lb. shoulder of lamb, boned and minced [ground]
2 onions, finely chopped
1 tablespoon chopped fresh parsley
1 teaspoon chopped fresh thyme
1 teaspoon salt
1 oz. [2 tablespoons] butter
2 tablespoons vegetable oil
1 small potato, finely chopped
1-inch piece of fresh root ginger, peeled and very finely chopped
1 teaspoon ground cumin
1 teaspoon ground coriander
½ teaspoon freshly ground black pepper
½ teaspoon sugar
½ teaspoon hot chilli powder
1 tablespoon white wine vinegar
⅛ teaspoon ground saffron, soaked in 2 tablespoons hot water
6 fl. oz. [¾ cup] water

Lancashire Hot Pot is a traditional favourite all over Britain.

In a large mixing bowl, combine the lamb, half the onions, the parsley, thyme and ½ teaspoon of the salt. Mix and knead the ingredients well. Shape the mixture into balls 1-inch in diameter.

In a large frying-pan, melt the butter with the oil over moderate heat. When the foam subsides, add the meatballs, a few at a time, and fry them, turning frequently, for 6 to 8 minutes, or until they are well browned. With a slotted spoon, transfer the meatballs to a plate.

In the same frying-pan, adding more oil and butter if necessary, fry the remaining onion and the potato, stirring occasionally, for 5 to 7 minutes or until the onion is soft and translucent but not brown and the potato is almost tender.

Add the ginger and cook, stirring occasionally, for 3 minutes. Add the cumin, coriander, pepper, sugar, chilli powder and the remaining salt and cook for 5 minutes, stirring frequently to prevent the spices from sticking to the bottom of the pan. Stir in the vinegar, saffron mixture and water. Reduce the heat to low and simmer for 2 minutes.

Return the meatballs to the pan and stir carefully to coat them with the spices. Cover the pan and simmer the mixture for 15 minutes or until the meatballs are just pink in the centre when broken open.

Remove the pan from the heat. Place the mixture on a serving dish and serve.

19

Whitsun Lamb

☆ ① ① ⧓ ⧓

A delicious combination of lamb and asparagus, Whitsun Lamb is an ideal lunch or supper dish. Serve with creamed potatoes.

4 SERVINGS

2 lb. asparagus, cooked and drained

2 lb. leg of lamb, cut into 2-inch cubes

2 oz. [½ cup] seasoned flour, made with 2 oz. [½ cup] flour, 1 teaspoon salt and ½ teaspoon black pepper

2 oz. [¼ cup] butter

2 medium-sized onions, thinly sliced

10 fl. oz. [1¼ cups] chicken stock

5 fl. oz. double cream [⅝ cup heavy cream]

1 teaspoon salt

1 teaspoon black pepper

juice of ½ lemon

With a sharp knife, cut off the asparagus tips and set them aside. Keep hot.

Place the stems in the jar of an electric blender and blend until they form a smooth purée. Set aside.

Roll the lamb cubes in the seasoned flour, shaking off any excess.

In a large flameproof casserole, melt the butter over moderate heat. When the foam subsides, add the onions and fry, stirring occasionally, for 5 to 7 minutes or until they are soft and translucent but not brown.

Add the lamb cubes and fry, stirring and turning occasionally, for 5 to 8 minutes or until they are lightly and evenly browned. Stir in the stock and bring the liquid to the boil. Reduce the

Serve Whitsun Lamb, a super blend of meat and asparagus, as a special treat for Sunday lunch!

heat to low and simmer the mixture for 50 minutes to 1 hour or until the meat is tender when pierced with the point of a sharp knife.

Remove the casserole from the heat and, with a slotted spoon, transfer the lamb cubes to a plate. Keep hot.

Stir the puréed asparagus and cream into the sauce in the casserole. Add the salt, pepper and lemon juice and cook, stirring frequently, for 3 to 5 minutes or until the sauce is thick and smooth.

Place the meat on a serving dish and pour the sauce around the meat. Garnish with the reserved asparagus tips and serve immediately.

20

Meatballs with Hot Mexican Sauce

☆   ①   ⊠

This recipe is for those who enjoy spicy food. Meatballs with Hot Mexican Sauce is an ideal dish for supper, served with noodles.

4-6 SERVINGS

MEATBALLS
2 lb. minced [ground] pork
1 large onion, finely grated
2 garlic cloves, crushed
2 oz. [⅓ cup] ground almonds
2 oz. [1 cup] fresh breadcrumbs
1 egg, lightly beaten
1 tablespoon chopped fresh parsley
¾ teaspoon ground cinnamon
½ teaspoon black pepper
1 teaspoon salt
3 tablespoons medium dry sherry
1 tablespoon butter
2 tablespoons olive oil
SAUCE
1 large onion, finely chopped
1 garlic clove, crushed

½ tablespoon soft brown sugar
6 medium-sized tomatoes, blanched, peeled, seeded and chopped
1 green pepper, white pith removed, seeded and sliced
1 red pepper, white pith removed, seeded and sliced
1 green chilli, finely chopped
¼ teaspoon cayenne pepper
1 teaspoon paprika
1 tablespoon chopped fresh parsley
5 fl. oz. [⅝ cup] beef stock
1 teaspoon salt
¼ teaspoon black pepper
2 teaspoons cornflour [cornstarch] dissolved in 4 tablespoons medium dry sherry

In a large mixing bowl, combine the pork, onion, garlic, almonds, breadcrumbs, egg, parsley, cinnamon, pepper, salt and sherry. Using your hands, mix and knead the ingredients well. Shape the meat mixture into about 36 walnut-sized balls.

In a large deep frying-pan, melt the butter with the oil over moderate heat. When the foam subsides, add the meatballs, a few at a time, and fry them, turning occasionally, for 6 to 8 minutes or until they are well browned. Transfer the meatballs to a plate. Set aside.

Add the onion, garlic and brown sugar to the frying-pan and fry, stirring occasionally, for 6 to 8 minutes, or until the onion is soft and golden brown. Add the tomatoes, green and red peppers, the chilli, cayenne, paprika and parsley and cook for 3 minutes, stirring occasionally.

Pour in the stock and season with the salt and pepper. Increase the heat to high and bring the mixture to the boil. Reduce the heat to low and stir in the cornflour [cornstarch] mixture. Add the meatballs to the sauce, cover the pan and continue cooking for a further 20 to 25 minutes or until the meatballs are thoroughly cooked.

Serve at once.

Meatballs with Hot Mexican Sauce will satisfy the whole family.

21

Near Eastern Pork with Peanuts and Grapes

☆   ①   ✄

Tender pork fillet, gently cooked with juicy grapes and sprinkled with toasted peanuts, Near Eastern Pork with Peanuts and Grapes is an exotic dish to serve at a special dinner party. If peanuts are not available, use any type of nut — although the flavour will, naturally, be slightly different.

6 SERVINGS

2 tablespoons peanut oil
2 lb. pork fillet, cut into 1-inch cubes
1 teaspoon salt
½ teaspoon black pepper
2½ oz. [½ cup] unsalted peanuts, ground
2 tablespoons soy sauce
¼ teaspoon mild chilli powder
1 lb. seedless white grapes, halved
2½ oz. [½ cup] unsalted peanuts, finely chopped and toasted

In a large frying-pan, heat the oil over moderate heat. When the oil is hot, add the pork cubes. Cook the pork, stirring and turning occasionally, for 6 to 8 minutes or until the cubes are lightly and evenly browned.

Add the salt, pepper, ground peanuts, soy sauce and chilli powder and mix well.

Exotic Near Eastern Pork with Peanuts and Grapes will provide a new - and delicious - taste experience for the family.

Reduce the heat to low. Add the grapes and simmer the mixture for 40 to 50 minutes, or until the pork is very tender when pierced with the point of a sharp knife.

Remove the pan from the heat and transfer the mixture to a warmed serving dish. Sprinkle with the chopped peanuts and serve at once.

Pork Casserole with Lemon

☆   ① ①   ✄ ✄

The lemon flavouring in this recipe counteracts the richness of the pork and enhances its flavour. Serve the casserole with jacket potatoes and steamed French beans. Pare the lemon rind in one piece so that it will be easy to remove.

8 SERVINGS

4 lb. pork fillet, cut into 1-inch cubes
2 oz. [½ cup] seasoned flour, made with 2 oz. [½ cup] flour, ½ teaspoon salt and ½ teaspoon black pepper
2 fl. oz. [¼ cup] olive oil

2 garlic cloves, crushed
3 medium-sized onions, roughly chopped
6 celery stalks, trimmed and cut into ½-inch lengths
1½ pints [3¾ cups] chicken stock
1 teaspoon dried marjoram
1 teaspoon dried chervil .
½ teaspoon dried thyme
finely pared rind and juice of 2 lemons
2 lemons, peeled, white pith removed, segmented and finely chopped
1 tablespoon butter blended with ½ tablespoon flour

Coat the pork cubes in the seasoned flour, shaking off any excess. Set aside.

In a very large flameproof casserole, heat the oil over moderate heat. When the oil is hot, add the garlic and onions and cook them, stirring occasionally, for 5 to 7 minutes or until the onions are soft and translucent but not brown. Using a slotted spoon, transfer the onions and garlic to a plate. Set aside.

Add the pork cubes to the pan, a few at a time, and fry them, turning them frequently, for 6 to 8 minutes or until they are lightly and evenly browned. With a slotted spoon, transfer the cubes to a plate as they brown.

Return the onions and garlic to the casserole. Add the celery and pour in the chicken stock. Increase the heat to high and bring the stock to the boil, stirring constantly. Add the pork cubes and, when the mixture comes to the boil again, reduce the heat to low. Stir in the marjoram, chervil, thyme, lemon rind and juice. Cover the casserole and simmer the meat for 50 minutes or until it is very tender when pierced with the point of a sharp knife.

Remove and discard the lemon rind. Increase the heat to moderate and stir in the lemon segments. Add the butter mixture, in small pieces, stirring constantly, making sure that each piece is absorbed before adding the next. Reduce the heat to low and simmer the sauce for 2 minutes, stirring frequently. Remove the casserole from the heat and serve immediately.

Pork Stew

☆   ①   ✗ ✗

A aelicious and inexpensive dinner dish, Pork Stew may be served with rice, courgettes grillées and a tomato salad. Some well-chilled white wine or lager would complement this dish very well.

4-6 SERVINGS

2 fl. oz. [¼ cup] vegetable oil
2 lb. lean pork fillet, cut into
   1-inch strips
1 medium-sized onion, thinly sliced
4 oz. mushrooms, wiped clean
   and sliced
3 celery stalks, trimmed and
   thinly sliced
1 tablespoon finely chopped
   orange rind
16 fl. oz. [2 cups] chicken stock
1 teaspoon curry powder
½ teaspoon salt
¼ teaspoon black pepper
2 teaspoons cornflour [cornstarch],
   dissolved in 3 tablespoons water
5 fl. oz. double cream [⅝ cup heavy
   cream]
2 teaspoons lemon juice

In a large flameproof casserole or saucepan, heat the oil over moderate heat. When the oil is hot, add the pork strips and cook them, turning occasionally, for 6 to 8 minutes, or until they are lightly and evenly browned. With a slotted spoon, transfer the pork to a bowl and set aside.

Add the onion to the casserole and cook, stirring occasionally, for 5 to 7 minutes, or until it is soft and translucent but not brown. Add the mushrooms, celery and orange rind. Add the stock and cook, stirring occasionally, for 3 to 5 minutes or until the stock has come to the boil. Stir in the curry powder, salt and pepper, and mix well to blend.

Return the pork to the casserole. Reduce the heat to low, cover the pan and simmer the mixture for 35 to 40 minutes, or until the pork is tender when pierced with a sharp knife.

Remove the pan from the heat and stir in the cornflour [cornstarch] mixture, stirring until it has dissolved. Stir in the cream and lemon juice and return the pan to low heat. Simmer the mixture gently for 2 to 3 minutes, or until the sauce is hot but not boiling.

Remove the pan from the heat and transfer the mixture to a warmed serving dish. Serve at once.

Spanish Pork Casserole

☆   ① ①   ✗ ✗

This flavourful Spanish Pork Casserole is ideal for an informal dinner or lunch. Serve it with saffron-flavoured rice for a really authentic touch!

6 SERVINGS

2 oz. [½ cup] seasoned flour, made
   with 2 oz. [½ cup] flour, ½ teaspoon
   salt and ¼ teaspoon black pepper
3 lb. lean pork fillet, cut into
   ¼-inch thick slices
4 tablespoons vegetable oil
2 medium-sized onions, sliced
2 garlic cloves, finely chopped
6 tomatoes, blanched, peeled,
   seeded and chopped
12 fl. oz. [1½ cups] dry white wine or
   chicken stock
1 teaspoon dried sweet basil
1 tablespoon chopped fresh parsley

Sprinkle the seasoned flour on to a plate. Coat the pork slices on both sides with the seasoned flour.

In a large frying-pan, heat the oil over moderate heat. When the oil is hot, add the pork slices and brown them for 4 minutes on each side. With tongs, transfer the slices from the pan to a flameproof casserole or saucepan.

Add the onions and garlic to the frying-pan and fry them for 8 to 10 minutes, or until they are golden brown.

Add the tomatoes, wine or stock and basil to the frying-pan and continue cooking for 2 to 3 minutes.

Pour the sauce over the meat. Cover the casserole or saucepan and place it over low heat. Simmer for 1 hour.

Remove the casserole from the heat and sprinkle the meat with parsley. Serve at once, from the casserole.

Serve Spanish Pork Casserole with saffron-flavoured rice for a really authentic Iberian touch!

Breast of Veal with Vegetables

☆ ① ① ✂

A relatively inexpensive dish, Breast of Veal with Vegetables is colourful and quick to make. Serve with mashed potatoes and crusty bread for a satisfying family meal.

6 SERVINGS

1 x 3 lb. breast of veal, trimmed of excess fat
3 tablespoons vegetable oil
½ teaspoon salt
½ teaspoon freshly ground black pepper
10 fl. oz. [1¼ cups] home-made chicken stock
12 oz. small fresh or frozen carrots, scraped and cut into ¼-inch slices
8 oz. fresh or frozen and thawed peas, weighed after shelling
1 teaspoon soft brown sugar

Place the meat on a board and, using a sharp knife, cut it into 2- by 3-inch pieces.

In a large frying-pan, heat the oil over moderate heat. When the oil is hot, add the meat and cook, turning once, for 8 to 10 minutes or until it is lightly browned all over. Remove the pan from the heat. Pour off and discard the oil in the pan. Return the pan to the heat and sprinkle over the salt and pepper and pour in the stock. Bring the liquid to the boil, add the carrots and reduce the heat to moderately low. Simmer the mixture for 15 minutes.

Add the peas and sugar to the pan and continue cooking for 15 to 20 minutes or until the meat is tender when pierced with the point of a sharp knife.

Remove the pan from the heat and pour the meat and vegetables into a warmed serving dish.

Serve immediately.

Curried Veal Stew

☆ ☆ ① ① ✂ ✂

Curried Veal Stew is a delicious way of preparing veal, and the spicy and creamy sauce gives the dish a delicate and subtle flavour. Serve with plain boiled rice and a tossed mixed salad. For special occasions, accompany it with dry white wine.

4 SERVINGS

2 lb. lean boned veal, cut into 1-inch cubes
1 teaspoon salt
1 teaspoon freshly ground black pepper
¼ teaspoon cayenne pepper
3 oz. [⅜ cup] butter
2 medium-sized onions, finely chopped
1 garlic clove, crushed
1 large tart apple, cored and chopped
2 celery stalks, trimmed and chopped
2 teaspoons curry powder
1 pint [2½ cups] chicken or veal stock
2 oz. [⅓ cup] sultanas or seedless raisins
2 tablespoons chopped blanched almonds
2 tablespoons double [heavy] cream
2 tablespoons cornflour [cornstarch] dissolved in 3 tablespoons chicken or veal stock

Place the veal on a working surface and rub in the salt, pepper and cayenne. Set aside.

Breast of Veal with Vegetables may be served with mashed potatoes and brown bread for a wholesome family meal.

White Meat Casserole is easy to make – and even easier to eat!

In a large flameproof casserole, melt the butter over moderate heat. When the foam subsides, add the onions and garlic and cook, stirring occasionally, for 5 to 7 minutes or until the onions are soft and translucent but not brown. Add the veal cubes and cook, turning and stirring, for 8 to 10 minutes or until they are evenly browned. Stir in the apple, celery and curry powder and mix well. Cook, stirring frequently, for 3 minutes. Pour over the stock and bring the liquid to the boil. Reduce the heat to low, cover and simmer the mixture for 40 minutes. Stir in the sultanas or seedless raisins and the almonds and continue to simmer the mixture for a further 20 minutes or until the meat is tender when pierced with the point of a sharp knife. Add the cream and cook for 1 minute.

Stir in the cornflour [cornstarch] mixture, and cook, stirring constantly, for 2 to 3 minutes or until the liquid has thickened. Remove the casserole from the heat and serve at once, straight from the casserole.

White Meat Casserole

☆　　　①　①　　　▷◁ ▷◁ ▷◁

A super way to prepare veal, White Meat Casserole is easy to make and tastes simply delicious served with rice and a crisp green salad. Accompany this dish with some well chilled white wine, such as Liebfraumilch, for a special treat.

6 SERVINGS

2 oz. [¼ cup] plus 2 tablespoons butter
1 medium-sized onion, finely chopped
3 lb. lean shoulder or breast of veal, cut into 1-inch cubes
28 fl. oz. [3½ cups] canned cream of mushroom soup
1 teaspoon paprika
¼ teaspoon grated nutmeg
1 teaspoon salt
½ teaspoon freshly ground white pepper
8 oz. button mushrooms, wiped clean and halved

Preheat the oven to moderate 350°F (Gas Mark 4, 180°C).

In a large flameproof casserole, melt the 2 ounces [¼ cup] of butter over moderate heat. When the foam subsides, add the onion and fry, stirring occasionally, for 5 to 7 minutes or until it is soft and translucent but not brown. Add the veal cubes and fry, stirring occasionally, for 6 to 8 minutes or until the meat is lightly browned all over. Pour over the soup. Season the mixture with the paprika, nutmeg, salt and pepper. Stir the ingredients together to mix well. Cover the casserole and transfer it to the oven. Cook the veal for 2 hours.

Meanwhile, in a small frying-pan, melt the remaining butter over moderate heat. When the foam subsides, add the mushrooms and fry, stirring constantly, for 3 minutes. Remove the pan from the heat and add the mushrooms to the casserole. Cook the mixture, covered, for a further 30 minutes or until the veal is very tender when pierced with the point of a sharp knife.

Remove the casserole from the oven. Serve immediately, straight from the casserole.

Brunswick Stew

This famous American stew, which is ideal for a family lunch or dinner, may be served with hot crusty bread.

4 SERVINGS

- 2 oz. [4 tablespoons] butter
- 8 chicken pieces
- 1 large onion, sliced
- 1 green pepper, white pith removed, seeded and coarsely chopped
- 10 fl. oz. [1¼ cups] chicken stock
- 14 oz. canned peeled tomatoes, drained
- ½ teaspoon salt
- ½ teaspoon cayenne pepper
- 1 tablespoon Worcestershire sauce
- 8 oz. canned and drained or frozen and thawed sweetcorn
- 1 lb. canned and drained or frozen and thawed lima beans or 1 lb. broad beans
- 1 tablespoon cornflour [cornstarch] mixed with 2 tablespoons water

In a flameproof casserole, heat the butter over moderate heat. Add the chicken pieces and fry them for 3 to 5 minutes on each side or until they are golden brown. Remove the chicken pieces and set them aside on a plate.

Add the onion and green pepper to the casserole and cook for 5 to 7 minutes, or until the onion is soft and translucent.

Add the stock, tomatoes, salt, cayenne and Worcestershire sauce. Stir to mix, return the chicken to the casserole and bring to the boil. Cover and reduce the heat to low. Simmer gently for 40 minutes.

Add the sweetcorn and lima or broad beans. Re-cover the casserole and continue to simmer for another 15 minutes.

Add the cornflour [cornstarch] mixture to the stew, stirring constantly. Cook, stirring, for 10 minutes.

Serve at once from the casserole.

Brunswick Stew is a colourful and tasty mixture of chicken pieces and various vegetables.

Duck Curry

A rich, spicy dish, Duck Curry is easy to make. Serve it with plain boiled rice, fresh home-made chutney and a tomato and onion salad.

4 SERVINGS

5 tablespoons vegetable oil
1 x 6 lb. duck, cut into serving
   pieces
1 teaspoon mustard seeds
3 medium-sized onions, finely
   chopped
2 garlic cloves, finely chopped
1½-inch piece root ginger, peeled
   and finely chopped
1 green chilli, finely chopped
1 teaspoon ground cumin
1 teaspoon hot chilli powder
1 tablespoon ground coriander
1 tablespoon garam masala
1 teaspoon turmeric
½ teaspoon salt
3 tablespoons vinegar
½-inch slice creamed coconut
10 fl. oz. [1¼ cups] boiling water

In a large saucepan, heat the oil over moderate heat. Add the duck pieces and fry them for 4 to 5 minutes on each side or until they are golden brown. Using tongs, remove the duck pieces as they brown and set them aside on a plate.

Add the mustard seeds, cover the pan and fry them for 2 minutes. Keep the pan covered or the mustard seeds will spatter. Remove the cover and add the onions. Fry them for 8 minutes or until they are golden brown. Add the garlic, ginger and green chilli and fry, stirring constantly, for 2 to 3 minutes.

Put the cumin, chilli powder, coriander, garam masala, turmeric and salt in a small bowl. Add the vinegar and mix well to make a paste. Add the paste to the sauce-pan and fry, stirring constantly, for 8 minutes.

This rich, hot Duck Curry is an authentic Indian dish. The spices used may be obtained from Oriental delicatessens.

Add the duck pieces and turn them over several times so that they are well coated with the spices. Continue frying for 2 to 3 minutes.

Meanwhile, in a small bowl, dissolve the creamed coconut in the water to make coconut milk. Pour the coconut milk over the duck pieces in the pan and stir to mix the coconut milk into the spices. Reduce the heat to moderately low, cover the pan and simmer for 40 minutes or until the duck is tender and the gravy thick.

Taste the curry and add more salt if necessary. Serve hot.

Offal

Liver with Olives and Mushrooms

☆   ①   ✕ ✕

A tasty and inexpensive meal, Liver with Olives and Mushrooms may be served with puréed potatoes and fresh peas cooked with mint.

4 SERVINGS

- 1 tablespoon vegetable oil
- 4 streaky bacon slices, chopped
- 4 medium-sized onions, finely chopped
- 4 oz. mushrooms, wiped clean and sliced
- 1½ oz. [3 tablespoons] butter
- 1 lb. pig's liver, trimmed and thinly sliced
- 12 fl. oz. [1½ cups] beef stock
- 1 teaspoon salt
- ½ teaspoon black pepper
- ½ teaspoon dried thyme
- 1 tablespoon cornflour [cornstarch] dissolved in 1 tablespoon water
- 12 green olives, halved and stoned
  juice of ½ lemon

Preheat the oven to moderate 350°F (Gas Mark 4, 180°C).

In a medium-sized frying-pan, heat the vegetable oil over moderate heat. When the oil is hot, add the bacon and cook, stirring and turning occasionally, for 3 minutes. Add the onions and cook, stirring occasionally, for 5 to 7 minutes, or until they are soft and translucent but not brown. Stir in the mushrooms and cook, stirring occasionally, for 3 minutes.

With a slotted spoon, transfer the bacon and vegetables to a medium-sized oven-proof casserole.

Add the butter to the oil remaining in the frying-pan and melt it over moderate heat. When the foam subsides, add the liver to the pan and cook, turning occasionally, for 5 to 6 minutes, or until the meat is lightly and evenly browned. With a slotted spoon, remove the meat from the pan and add it to the casserole.

Pour the stock into the frying-pan and add the salt, pepper and thyme. Bring the liquid to the boil, stirring and scraping in any brown bits adhering to the bottom. Stir in the cornflour [cornstarch] mixture and cook, stirring constantly, for 1 minute, or until the liquid has thickened and is smooth. Remove the pan from the heat and pour the mixture into the casserole.

Stir in the olives and lemon juice and place the casserole in the oven. Bake for 1 to 1¼ hours, or until the meat is tender when pierced with the point of a sharp knife.

Remove the casserole from the oven and serve at once.

Oxtail Casserole

☆   ① ①   ✕ ✕ ✕

Oxtail is a comparatively inexpensive cut of meat, and when cooked in this manner makes a delightful, rich dish for the family. Serve the meat on the bones; however, if you are serving the oxtail at a dinner party, remove the meat from the bones. Serve Oxtail Casserole with a mixture of sautéed root vegetables, chipolata sausages and buttered noodles.

4 SERVINGS

- 1 oxtail, skinned and cut into pieces
- ½ teaspoon salt
- ½ teaspoon freshly ground black pepper
- ¼ teaspoon mixed spice or ground allspice
- 1 tablespoon brandy
- 1 oz. [2 tablespoons] butter
- 2 medium-sized onions, finely chopped
- 2 medium-sized carrots, scraped and chopped
  bouquet garni, consisting of 4 parsley sprigs, 1 thyme spray and 1 bay leaf tied together
- 6 fl. oz. [¾ cup] home-made beef stock
- 6 fl. oz. [¾ cup] dry red wine
- 2 tablespoons tomato purée

Place the oxtail pieces on a plate and rub them all over with the salt, pepper and mixed spice or allspice. Pour over the brandy and set the pieces aside for 20 minutes.

In a large, flameproof casserole, melt the butter over moderate heat. When the foam subsides, add the oxtail pieces and fry them, turning frequently, for 5 minutes or until they are evenly browned.

Using tongs or a slotted spoon, transfer the oxtail pieces to a plate and keep warm.

Add the onions and carrots to the casserole and cook them, stirring occasionally, for 5 to 7 minutes or until the onions are soft and translucent but not brown. Return the oxtail pieces to the casserole and add the bouquet garni, stock, wine and tomato purée. The liquid should almost cover the meat so add a little more stock if necessary.

Bring the liquid to the boil, skimming off any scum that rises to the surface. Cover the casserole and reduce the heat to very low. Simmer the oxtail for 4 hours or until the meat is very tender and comes away from the bones. Remove and discard the bouquet garni.

Remove the casserole from the heat and set it aside to cool completely. Place the casserole in the refrigerator to chill for at least 8 hours or overnight.

Remove the casserole from the refrig-

This delicious Oxtail Casserole makes an inexpensive and satisfying supper for the family.

erator. Remove and discard the fat that has risen to the surface.

Place the casserole over moderate heat and bring the liquid slowly to the boil. Reduce the heat to low and simmer for 10 minutes. Using a slotted spoon, transfer the oxtail pieces to a heated serving dish. Keep warm.

Increase the heat to moderately high and boil the braising liquid until it has reduced by about one-third. Remove the pan from the heat. Pour a little of the

braising liquid over the oxtail pieces and pour the remainder into a warmed sauceboat.

Serve immediately.

Paprika Vegetable and Sausage Stew

☆　　　①　　　⊠

A tasty adaptation of a traditional Hungarian dish, Paprika Vegetable and Sausage Stew is a meal in itself.

4 SERVINGS

2 fl. oz. [¼ cup] vegetable oil
2 onions, finely chopped
2 garlic cloves, crushed
1 green pepper, white pith removed, seeded and chopped
1 red pepper, white pith removed, seeded and chopped
1 tablespoon paprika
½ teaspoon salt
¼ teaspoon black pepper
½ teaspoon dried dill
1 lb. canned peeled tomatoes
1 lb. potatoes, cooked and sliced
8 oz. garlic sausage, chopped
5 fl. oz. [⅝ cup] sour cream

In a medium-sized flameproof casserole, heat the oil over moderate heat. When the oil is hot, add the onions and garlic and cook, stirring occasionally, for 5 to 7

minutes or until the onions are soft and translucent but not brown. Add the green and red peppers and cook, stirring occasionally, for a further 5 minutes.

Remove the casserole from the heat and stir in the paprika, salt, pepper, dill and the tomatoes with the can juice mixing well to blend.

Return the casserole to low heat and simmer the mixture for 25 to 30 minutes or until the vegetables are tender. Stir in the potatoes, sausage and sour cream and simmer over low heat for a further 5 minutes or until the potatoes and sausage are heated through.

Remove the casserole from the heat and serve at once.

Daube de Lapin
RABBIT STEW

Daube de Lapin is not one of the great French daubes but it is, nevertheless, a popular and quite economical version of the classic beef daubes. Served with mashed potatoes and green vegetables, it makes a richly sustaining winter meal.

6 SERVINGS

1 x 3 lb. rabbit, cut into serving
   pieces
8 oz. streaky bacon slices, cut into
   2-inch strips
2 onions, thinly sliced
1 garlic clove, finely chopped
3 carrots, scraped and thinly sliced
MARINADE
16 fl. oz. [2 cups] dry white wine
1 tablespoon olive oil
1 teaspoon salt
6 black peppercorns
2 parsley sprigs
1 bay leaf
2 garlic cloves, crushed
$\frac{1}{2}$ teaspoon dried thyme

In a large shallow bowl, combine all the marinade ingredients together and stir well to mix. Add the rabbit pieces and baste them thoroughly. Cover the dish and leave the rabbit to marinate overnight, or for at least 12 hours.

Remove the rabbit pieces from the marinade and dry them on kitchen paper towels. Strain the marinade into a jug and reserve it. Remove the bay leaf.

Preheat the oven to moderate 350°F (Gas Mark 4, 180°C).

An adaptation of a classic French dish, Daube de Lapin makes an exciting dish for a special occasion.

In a large, flameproof casserole, fry the bacon strips over moderate heat until they are quite crisp. With a slotted spoon remove the bacon pieces from the pan and drain them on kitchen paper towels.

Add the onions, garlic and carrots to the fat in the casserole and cook them for 5 to 6 minutes, or until they are lightly coloured. Add the rabbit pieces and turn frequently to brown them evenly and quickly. If there is not enough fat in the pan, add a little butter or oil.

Add the reserved marinade to the casserole and bring the liquid to the boil.

Remove the casserole from the heat, add the bacon pieces to the mixture and place the casserole in the oven. Braise for 1 hour, or until the rabbit is tender. Remove from the oven and serve.

Lamb Stew with Sherry

Lamb Stew with Sherry is a flavourful Spanish dish in which pieces of lamb are marinated in sherry.

6 SERVINGS

10 fl. oz. [1$\frac{1}{4}$ cups] dry sherry
2 garlic cloves, crushed
3 lb. boned lamb, cut into 2-inch
   pieces
1 teaspoon salt
$\frac{1}{2}$ teaspoon black pepper
1 teaspoon ground cumin
4 tablespoons vegetable oil
2 medium-sized onions, sliced
2 tablespoons flour

Combine the sherry and garlic in a large mixing bowl. Add the pieces of lamb, and mix well. Cover the bowl and leave the meat to marinate for 3 hours.

Remove the lamb from the marinade. Drain well and dry the meat on kitchen paper towels. Reserve the marinade.

Sprinkle the salt, pepper and cumin over the lamb.

In a large saucepan, heat the oil over moderate heat. Add the pieces of lamb and fry them for 3 to 5 minutes or until they are brown. Add the onions and fry for 3 minutes.

Add the flour and mix it well with the lamb and onions. Pour over the reserved marinade and, stirring constantly, bring to the boil.

Cover the saucepan and reduce the heat to moderately low. Simmer the stew for at least 1 hour, or until the lamb is tender. Serve very hot.

Sautéed Kidneys with Chipolatas and Wine

This is a superb informal dinner dish. Serve with creamed potatoes and buttered broccoli.

4 SERVINGS

2 oz. [$\frac{1}{4}$ cup] butter
12 lambs' kidneys, cleaned, and halved
4 pork chipolata sausages, twisted
   and halved
1 tablespoon flour
4 fl. oz. [$\frac{1}{2}$ cup] red wine
8 fl. oz. [1 cup] beef stock
1 tablespoon tomato purée
2 tablespoons brandy
$\frac{1}{2}$ teaspoon salt
$\frac{1}{2}$ teaspoon black pepper
12 button (pearl) onions, blanched
2 teaspoons chopped fresh parsley

In a large frying-pan, melt the butter over moderate heat. When the foam subsides, add the kidneys and chipolata halves to the pan. Cook them, stirring frequently, for 8 minutes or until the kidneys are tender and the chipolatas are lightly browned. With a slotted spoon, transfer the kidneys and chipolatas to a plate.

Remove the pan from the heat and stir in the flour with a wooden spoon. Return the pan to the heat and cook the mixture for 30 seconds. Gradually add the wine and stock, stirring constantly. Bring the mixture to the boil, stirring occasionally. Add the tomato purée, brandy, salt and pepper, stirring constantly. Return the kidneys and chipolatas to the pan and add the onions. Reduce the heat to low, cover the pan and cook the mixture for 25 minutes, stirring occasionally.

Remove the pan from the heat and transfer the contents to a warmed serving dish. Sprinkle over the parsley and serve.

Sautéed Kidneys with Chipolatas and Wine makes a superb dinner dish.

Spanish Beef Stew with Rice, Tomatoes and Herbs

☆　　　①　①　　✕　✕　✕

A delicious stew from the Spanish border country on the Mediterranean coast, Spanish Beef Stew with Rice, Tomatoes and Herbs may be served with a green salad, French bread and a young red wine, such as Beaujolais.

6 SERVINGS

2 slices streaky bacon, diced
1 pint [2½ cups] water
2 tablespoons olive oil
3 lb. stewing steak, cut into 1-inch thick 2½-inch squares
2 medium-sized onions, sliced
8 oz. [1⅓ cups] long-grain rice
10 fl. oz. [1¼ cups] dry white wine
15 fl. oz. [1⅞ cups] beef stock
½ teaspoon salt
¼ teaspoon black pepper
2 garlic cloves, crushed
¼ teaspoon dried thyme
¼ teaspoon dried basil
¼ teaspoon dried oregano
⅛ teaspoon ground saffron
1 bay leaf
1 lb. ripe tomatoes, blanched, peeled, seeded and roughly chopped
4 oz. [1 cup] Gruyère or Parmesan cheese, grated

Preheat the oven to warm 325°F (Gas Mark 3, 170°C).

Place the diced bacon in a medium-sized pan and cover with the water. Bring the water to the boil over moderate heat. Reduce the heat and simmer gently for 10 minutes. Drain off the water and dry the bacon on kitchen paper towels.

In a heavy, large frying-pan, heat the oil over moderate heat and add the bacon. Fry the bacon for 3 minutes, turning it several times so that it browns. Remove the bacon with a slotted spoon and put it in a large flameproof casserole.

Dry the meat on kitchen paper towels. Over moderate heat, reheat the oil in the frying-pan until it is very hot. Quickly brown the meat a few pieces at a time. With a slotted spoon, transfer the pieces of meat as they brown to the casserole.

Reduce the heat to moderately low, add the onions to the pan and fry them lightly for 5 minutes, stirring occasionally. Remove the onions with a slotted spoon and add them to the casserole. Add the rice to the frying-pan, still using the same fat, and stir and cook for 2 to 3 minutes, or until the rice looks milky. Turn the rice into a medium-sized bowl.

Add the wine to the frying-pan, stir for 1 minute to dissolve the coagulated juices and pour the liquid into the casserole. Add the stock to the casserole

Spanish Beef Stew with Rice, Tomatoes and Herbs is surprisingly easy to make - and looks and tastes delicious. Serve with salad.

and place it over moderate heat. Stir in the salt, pepper, garlic, thyme, basil, oregano, saffron and bay leaf. Bring the liquid to the boil. Cover the casserole and place it in the lower part of the oven. Leave to cook for 1 hour.

Remove the casserole from the oven, stir in the tomatoes, bring to the boil on top of the stove, cover and return the casserole to the oven for an additional 2 hours, or until the meat is tender when pierced with a fork.

Tilt the casserole and skim off the fat. Stir the rice into the casserole. Place the casserole on top of the stove and bring the liquid to the boil over moderate heat.

Raise the oven heat to fairly hot 375°F (Gas Mark 5, 190°C).

Return the casserole to the lower part of the oven. Cook for 20 minutes, or until the rice is tender and the liquid is absorbed.

Remove the casserole from the oven, taste and add more salt and pepper if necessary. Remove the bay leaf. Stir the cheese into the mixture and serve.

Soups and stews for entertaining

The first half of the book concentrated on the basics — those useful dishes that the family will happily eat till Kingdom come and that won't break the budget every time you even contemplate cooking them.

But entertaining is part of living, too, whether it be family, friends or just an end-of-the-week, whoopee-it's-payday binge and the recipes in this section therefore concentrate on luscious-to-look-at, easy-to-cook classics absolutely guaranteed to vastly impress any guests lucky enough to sample them — just check the recipes for Boeuf Bourguinonne (page 48), Vichyssoise (page 44) or the colourful Danish Chicken Casserole (pictured above, recipe page 62) if you need convincing!

Most are a bit more expensive than the 'family-type' recipes (everyone, after all, longs for, and needs, the occasional bit of caviar on a beer budget!) but for those occasions when the boss and his wife are definitely, unputoffably coming to dinner and payday is still a long way off, we've constructed some less expensive, but still festive, dishes in **For Budget Occasions.**

Like the first section, all of the recipes on the following pages are specially chosen for their flexibility and the fact that almost all their preparation can be done ahead of time, as well as for their delicious taste. All make nourishing meals for ANY occasion, and without wearing you to a frazzle cooking them. So — try them, enjoy them — and good eating!

Asparagus Cream Soup

This delicious soup is made with fresh asparagus, cream and eggs. You can hasten the making process by using commercial vegetable stock, but the home-made stock given below tastes infinitely better and is well worth preparing.

4 SERVINGS

2 lb. asparagus
1 small onion, thinly sliced
10 fl. oz. [1¼ cups] water
1 teaspoon salt
½ teaspoon white pepper
1 oz. [4 tablespoons] flour
1 oz. [2 tablespoons] butter
2 egg yolks
5 fl. oz. single cream [⅝ cup light cream]

STOCK

1 oz. [2 tablespoons] butter
1 lb. carrots, scraped and chopped
1 lb. onions, thinly sliced
4 celery stalks, trimmed and chopped
1 small turnip, peeled and chopped
6 peppercorns
  bouquet garni, consisting of 4 parsley sprigs, 1 thyme spray and 1 bay leaf tied together
1 teaspoon salt
5 pints [6¼ pints] hot water

First, make the stock. In a large saucepan, melt the butter over moderate heat. When the foam subsides, add the carrots, onions, celery and turnip to the pan and cook, stirring occasionally, for 5 to 7 minutes or until the onions are soft and translucent but not brown. Add the peppercorns, bouquet garni, salt and hot water. Bring the water to the boil, half-cover the pan, reduce the heat to low and simmer the stock for 2 hours or until it has been reduced to about 1½ pints [3¾ cups].

Remove the pan from the heat and pour the stock through a strainer into a large jug, pressing down on the vegetables with the back of a wooden spoon to extract all the liquid. Set aside.

Trim and wash the asparagus. With a sharp knife, cut off 2 inches from the tips and set them aside. Peel the stalks and cut them into 1-inch lengths.

Place the sliced onion and asparagus stalks in a medium-sized saucepan. Add the strained stock and place the pan over low heat. Simmer the soup for 30 minutes.

Meanwhile, put the water and ½ teaspoon of salt into another saucepan. Place it over moderate heat and bring the water to the boil. Drop in the asparagus tips and boil for 5 to 8 minutes

or until they are tender. Drain the tips and set aside.

Pour the asparagus stock through a fine strainer into a medium-sized bowl. With the back of a wooden spoon, rub the asparagus stalks and onion through the strainer. Rinse and wipe dry the saucepan and pour back the stock. Reheat, adding the remaining salt, and the white pepper.

Roll the flour and butter together and work them into a soft paste. Roll the mixture into small balls.

Remove the stock from the heat and add the butter and flour balls, one at a time, stirring constantly with a wooden spoon. When the stock is thoroughly blended and smooth, place the pan over moderate heat and cook, stirring constantly until it boils. Remove the stock from the heat.

In a medium-sized bowl, beat the egg yolks and stir in the cream. Stirring constantly, add 10 fluid ounces [1¼ cups] of hot stock. Stirring constantly, pour the mixture into the remaining stock and replace the pan over very low heat. Simmer the soup, whisking constantly, for 2 minutes. Do not allow it to boil.

Remove the pan from the heat and pour the soup into a large, warmed tureen. Decorate with the reserved asparagus tips and serve at once.

Borscht

BEETROOT [BEET] SOUP

This is a classic summer Borscht, a light soup that is usually served hot. It is traditionally served hot with boiled potatoes as well as with sour cream. This recipe can be varied by whisking two beaten eggs into the hot soup just before serving.

6 SERVINGS

5 large raw beetroots [beets], peeled and coarsely grated
3 pints [7½ cups] water
1 onion, chopped
3 oz. tomato purée
1 tablespoon lemon juice
1 teaspoon salt
½ teaspoon black pepper
1 teaspoon sugar
10 fl. oz. [1¼ cups] sour cream

Place the beetroots [beets], water and onion in a large saucepan over high heat. Bring the liquid to the boil, cover the pan, reduce the heat to low and simmer for 45 minutes.

Add the tomato purée, lemon juice, salt, pepper and sugar to the saucepan. Cover and cook the soup over moderately low heat for 45 minutes.

Remove the pan from the heat. Strain the soup into a soup tureen, discarding the vegetables. Serve topped with spoonfuls of sour cream.

Cod Bouillabaisse

This simplified version of bouillabaisse is made only with cod, unlike the classic Mediterranean version, but it tastes just as good. The fish and potatoes are served separately from the soup, so that the dish is almost a meal in itself.

6-8 SERVINGS

3 tablespoons olive oil
3 onions, chopped
3 garlic cloves, crushed
4 large tomatoes, blanched, peeled and chopped
4 pints [5 pints] water
½ teaspoon crushed saffron threads
  bouquet garni, consisting of 4 parsley sprigs, 1 thyme spray and 1 bay leaf tied together
1 teaspoon grated orange rind
½ teaspoon cayenne pepper
½ teaspoon black pepper
½ teaspoon salt
10 potatoes, peeled and sliced into ½-inch rounds
2 lb. cod fillets, cut into chunks

In a large saucepan, heat the oil over moderate heat. When the oil is hot, add the onions and garlic and cook, stirring frequently, for 7 minutes. Add the tomatoes, stir to mix and cook for another 2 minutes. Stir in the water, saffron, bouquet garni, orange rind, cayenne, black pepper and salt. Reduce the heat to very low and simmer the soup for 20 minutes.

Drop the potato slices into the soup and cook for 10 minutes. Add the pieces of cod and cook, stirring occasionally, for another 15 minutes, or until the fish is cooked.

With a slotted spoon, remove the fish and potatoes from the soup and place them on a heated dish. Pour the soup through a strainer into a large, warmed tureen, pressing the vegetables and flavourings with the back of a wooden spoon to extract as much of their juices as possible. Discard the vegetables and flavourings.

Serve immediately.

A delicious, rich, creamy soup, Asparagus Cream Soup is not difficult to make and is fit to grace the finest table. Serve as a very special first course for a dinner party.

Cold Fruit Soup

☆   ①   ⋈ ⋈

Fruit soup makes a delicious, cooling first course for a summer's meal. Any fruit may be used, but a mixture of tart and sweet fruit makes a particularly good soup. Fruit soup may be served with whipped or sour cream.

4 SERVINGS

2 lb. mixed fruit, washed, peeled and chopped
2 oz. [¼ cup] sugar
⅛ teaspoon salt
1 clove
1 x 2-inch cinnamon stick
    juice and finely grated rind of 1 lemon
2 pints [5 cups] water

Place the fruit in a medium-sized saucepan. Add the sugar, salt, clove, cinnamon stick and lemon juice and lemon rind. Pour in the water and bring the mixture to the boil over moderately high heat, stirring occasionally. Reduce the heat to low, cover the pan and cook the fruit for

Cold Fruit Soup makes a refreshing first course for a summer meal. Or you could serve it as a very different, and light, dessert.

10 to 15 minutes, or until it is tender but still firm.

Remove and discard the cinnamon stick.

Strain the contents of the pan into a large serving bowl, rubbing the fruit through the strainer with the back of a wooden spoon. Discard any pulp remaining in the strainer. Set the soup aside to cool for 15 minutes.

Then place the bowl in the refrigerator and chill the soup for 1 hour before serving.

Vegetable Consommé

☆ ☆   ① ①   ⋈

This light and elegant soup is a simple variation on the classic consommé. It is easy to make and is a good starter when

followed by a rather rich   and   heavy main course.

4 SERVINGS

1 oz. [2 tablespoons] butter
2 small carrots, scraped and finely diced
1 small turnip, peeled and finely diced
2 leeks, white part only, cleaned and finely diced
1 small celery stalk, trimmed and finely diced
½ teaspoon salt
¼ teaspoon freshly ground black pepper
1 tablespoon green peas
2 pints [5 cups] strong clarified meat bouillon
3 fl. oz. [⅜ cup] sherry
1 teaspoon fresh chervil or ½ teaspoon dried chervil

In a medium-sized saucepan, melt the butter over moderate heat. When the foam subsides, add the carrots, turnip, leeks and celery and stir well with a wooden spoon. Add the salt and pepper.

36

Reduce the heat to low, cover the pan and cook for 5 minutes.

Add the peas and 5 fluid ounces [⅝ cup] of the bouillon and cook for a further 20 minutes.

Add the remaining bouillon to the pan with the sherry. Increase the heat to moderately high, stir the soup and bring it to the boil. Boil for 2 minutes. Pour the soup into a large, warmed tureen or individual serving bowls and sprinkle the chervil on top.

Serve at once.

Gazpacho

☆   ① ①   ⧗ ⧗

A classic Spanish soup, cold Gazpacho makes a refreshing summer lunch served with croûtons, small bowls of chopped olives, cucumbers, hard-boiled eggs and onion. Each guest then sprinkles his soup with a little of these accompaniments. It is easiest to make this soup with an electric blender.

4 SERVINGS

3 slices of brown bread, cut into 1-inch cubes
10 fl. oz. [1¼ cups] canned tomato juice
2 garlic cloves, finely chopped
½ cucumber, peeled and finely chopped
1 medium-sized green pepper, white pith removed, seeded and finely chopped
1 medium-sized red pepper, white pith removed, seeded and finely chopped
1 medium-sized onion, finely chopped
1½ lb. tomatoes, blanched, peeled, seeded and chopped
3 fl. oz. [⅜ cup] olive oil
2 tablespoons red wine vinegar
½ teaspoon salt
¼ teaspoon freshly ground black pepper
½ teaspoon fresh marjoram or ¼ teaspoon dried marjoram
½ teaspoon fresh basil or ¼ teaspoon dried basil
4 ice cubes [optional]

This exotic recipe for Gazpacho originated in Spain but is now enjoyed throughout the world. Serve with the accompaniments pictured here.

Place the bread cubes in a medium-sized mixing bowl and pour over the tomato juice. Leave the bread cubes to soak for 5 minutes, then squeeze them carefully to extract the excess juice. Transfer them to a large mixing bowl. Reserve the tomato juice.

Add the chopped garlic, cucumber, peppers, onion and tomatoes to the soaked bread cubes and stir to mix thoroughly. Purée the ingredients by pounding them in a mortar with a pestle to a paste and then rubbing them through a strainer, or by putting them through a food mill. Stir in the reserved tomato juice. If you are using a blender, purée all of the vegetables and bread cubes with the reserved tomato juice.

Add the oil, vinegar, salt, pepper, marjoram and basil to the purée and stir well. The soup should be the consistency of single [light] cream, so add more tomato juice if necessary.

Turn the soup into a deep serving bowl and place it in the refrigerator to chill for at least 1 hour.

Just before serving, stir the soup well and drop in the ice cubes, if you are using them.

Serve the Gazpacho immediately.

Greek Egg and Lemon Soup

☆ ☆   ①   ⋈

This traditional soup has an unusual lemon flavour. Serve as a first course to a special dinner.

6 SERVINGS

3 pints [7½ cups] chicken stock
3 oz. [½ cup] long-grain rice, washed, soaked in cold water for 30 minutes and drained
4 eggs
juice of 2 lemons
¼ teaspoon freshly ground black pepper
1 tablespoon finely chopped fresh parsley

Put the stock in a large saucepan and bring it to the boil. Add the rice and simmer over low heat for 15 to 20 minutes, or until the rice is tender. Remove the pan from the heat.

Break the eggs into a medium-sized mixing bowl and beat with a wire whisk until they are light and fluffy.

Gradually add the lemon juice, beating constantly. Add a few spoonfuls of stock, a little at a time, beating constantly until it is well mixed. Carefully stir this mixture into the saucepan containing the rest of the stock.

Continue to cook the soup over moderate heat for 2 minutes. Do not let it boil or it will curdle. Add the pepper, sprinkle over the chopped parsley and serve immediately.

Haricot Bean Cream Soup

☆ ☆   ① ①   ⋈

A thick, rich soup, Haricot Bean Cream Soup is an ideal light supper dish. Serve with crispbreads and cheese for a delightful meal.

8 SERVINGS

5 oz. [⅝ cup] butter
2 oz. [½ cup] flour
2 pints [5 cups] chicken stock
1 pint [2½ cups] chicken consommé
12 oz. white haricot beans, soaked in cold water overnight, drained, cooked and puréed
1 teaspoon salt
1 teaspoon freshly ground black pepper
8 fl. oz. single cream [1 cup light cream]
6 egg yolks, lightly beaten

In a large saucepan, melt 2 ounces [¼ cup]

of the butter over moderate heat. Remove the pan from the heat. Stir in the flour until the mixture forms a thick paste. Gradually add the stock, stirring constantly and being careful to avoid lumps. Return the pan to the heat and cook, stirring constantly, for 2 to 3 minutes or until the soup is thick and smooth. Stir in the consommé, then the bean purée. Season with the salt and pepper. Cook, stirring constantly, for a further 3 minutes.

Stir in the cream and the remaining butter. Place the egg yolks in a small mixing bowl. Using a kitchen fork, beat in 4 tablespoons of the hot soup. Stir the egg yolk mixture into the soup. Reduce the heat to low and cook, stirring constantly, for a further 10 minutes. Do not allow the soup to come to the boil or the egg yolks will scramble.

Remove the pan from the heat. Ladle the soup into a large, warmed soup tureen or individual soup bowls and serve at once.

This traditional Greek Egg and Lemon Soup makes a colourful and elegant start to a meal. The soup has a distinctively lemon flavour.

Hungarian Apricot Soup

☆ ① ① ① ✕ ✕ ✕

An unusual soup made from apricots, chicken, wine and sour cream, Hungarian Apricot Soup may be served as a first course or as a light summer lunch.

4 SERVINGS

4 oz. [⅔ cup] dried apricots, chopped
10 fl. oz. [1¼ cups] dry white wine
1 oz. [2 tablespoons] butter
1 garlic clove, crushed
2 tablespoons flour
1 pint [2½ cups] chicken stock
4 oz. cooked chicken, diced
1 tablespoon chopped fresh chives
½ teaspoon salt
¼ teaspoon black pepper
⅛ teaspoon grated nutmeg
5 fl. oz. [⅝ cup] sour cream

Soak the apricots in the wine for 6 hours.

In a large saucepan, melt the butter over moderate heat. When the foam subsides, add the garlic and cook, stirring occasionally, for 4 minutes.

Remove the pan from the heat. With a wooden spoon, stir in the flour to make a smooth paste. Add the stock, stirring constantly. Stir in the apricots, wine, chicken, chives, salt, pepper and nutmeg.

Set the pan over high heat and bring the soup to the boil, stirring constantly.

Reduce the heat to low, cover the pan and simmer the soup, stirring occasionally, for 30 minutes.

Remove the pan from the heat. Stir in the sour cream. Pour the soup into a warmed soup tureen or individual soup bowls and serve immediately.

Manhattan Clam Chowder

☆ ① ✕

One of the most popular of American chowders, Manhattan Clam Chowder traditionally contains tomatoes, potatoes, thyme and, in some recipes, salt pork. Serve the chowder as a light lunch or dinner, with crusty bread or rolls and butter.

6 SERVINGS

4 oz. salt pork, diced
1 medium-sized onion, chopped
4 large tomatoes, blanched, peeled, seeded and coarsely chopped
3 medium-sized potatoes, diced
½ teaspoon black pepper
½ teaspoon salt
½ teaspoon dried thyme
5 fl. oz. [⅝ cup] tomato juice
1 pint [2½ cups] water
5 fl. oz. [⅝ cup] clam liquid
24 small clams, steamed, removed from their shells and finely chopped or 1 lb. canned clams, drained and with the juice reserved

Manhattan Clam Chowder is one of the most popular of the traditional American soups. Served with crusty rolls it's almost a meal in itself.

In a large, heavy saucepan, fry the salt pork over moderate heat for 5 to 8 minutes, or until it has rendered its fat and is golden brown. Scrape the bottom of the pan frequently with a wooden spoon to prevent the pork from sticking.

With a slotted spoon, remove the salt pork from the pan and set aside.

Add the onion to the pan and fry, stirring occasionally, for 5 to 7 minutes, or until it is soft and translucent but not brown.

Add the chopped tomatoes, potatoes, pepper, salt and thyme. Stir in the tomato juice, water and the clam liquid. Return the salt pork to the pan and bring the soup to the boil, stirring constantly.

Reduce the heat to low, cover the pan and simmer for 15 minutes, or until the potatoes are just tender when pierced with the point of a sharp knife.

Add the clams and cook, stirring, for a further 4 to 5 minutes, or until they are heated through. Taste the chowder and add a little more salt if necessary.

Remove the pan from the heat. Pour the soup into a warmed soup tureen or individual soup bowls and serve.

39

Mexican Chicken and Bean Soup

☆ ① ① ① ✕ ✕ ✕

The ingredients for this soup may surprise you, but the blend of flavours is delicious. It is a meal in itself, accompanied by crusty bread or — to be really authentic — hot tortillas.

6 SERVINGS

1 x 5 lb. boiling chicken
1 medium-sized onion, quartered
1 carrot, scraped and sliced
2 teaspoons salt
4 peppercorns
   bouquet garni, consisting of 4 parsley sprigs, 1 thyme spray and 1 bay leaf tied together
5 pints [6¼ pints] water
2 green peppers, white pith removed, seeded and sliced
1 large onion, sliced and pushed out into rings
14 oz. canned chick-peas, drained
¼ teaspoon black pepper
8 oz. Wensleydale or any white cheese, cubed
1 avocado, peeled, stoned, sliced and sprinkled with lemon juice

Put the chicken in a large saucepan with the quartered onion, carrot, 1 teaspoon of salt, the peppercorns and bouquet garni. Pour over the water, adding more if necessary to cover the chicken completely.

Place the saucepan over high heat. Bring the liquid to the boil and reduce the heat to moderately low. Simmer the chicken for 2 hours or until it is tender.

Remove the chicken from the pan. Set it on a board and cover it with aluminium foil to keep it warm.

Increase the heat under the saucepan to moderately high and bring the liquid back to the boil. Boil it for 15 minutes to reduce it slightly. Then strain the liquid, discarding the vegetables and seasonings. Rinse out the saucepan and return the liquid to it.

Bring the liquid back to the boil, using a metal spoon to skim off any fat that rises to the surface. Add the sliced green peppers and onion rings. Reduce the heat to moderately low and simmer for 10 minutes. Then add the chick-peas and continue simmering for 5 minutes.

While the chick-peas, peppers and onions are cooking, cut the chicken into serving pieces. Return the chicken pieces to the saucepan. Add the remaining 1 teaspoon salt and the pepper, and cook the soup for 5 minutes longer or until the chicken pieces are heated through. Stir in the cheese. As soon as the cheese begins to melt, transfer the soup to a warmed tureen. Add the avocado slices and serve.

Minestrone

☆ ① ① ✕ ✕ ✕

A nourishing Italian vegetable and pasta soup, Minestrone is easily made. It makes a hearty meal on its own, served with crisp rolls and butter. The vegetables and dried beans used in this recipe are the traditional ingredients but they can be varied according to taste.

8 SERVINGS

1½ pints [3¾ cups] water
4 oz. [½ cup] dried red kidney beans

Chicken, chick-peas, green peppers and cheese are the principal ingredients in this delightfully unusual soup which originated in Mexico.

2 oz. [¼ cup] dried chick-peas
6 oz. salt pork, cut into cubes
4 tablespoons olive oil
2 medium-sized onions, finely chopped
1 garlic clove, crushed or finely chopped
2 medium-sized potatoes, peeled and diced
4 carrots, scraped and cut into ½-inch lengths
4 celery stalks, trimmed and cut into ½-inch lengths
½ small cabbage, coarse outer leaves removed, washed and finely shredded
6 medium-sized tomatoes, blanched, peeled, seeded and coarsely chopped
4 pints [5 pints] chicken stock

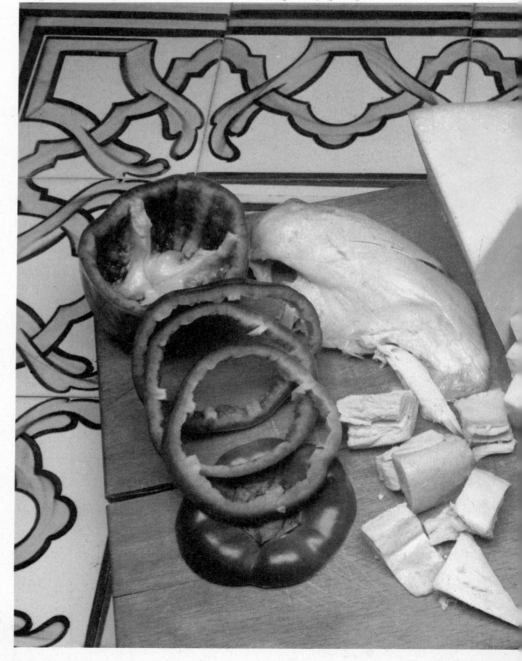

40

bouquet garni, consisting of 4 parsley sprigs, 1 thyme spray and 1 bay leaf tied together
½ teaspoon salt
1 teaspoon freshly ground black pepper
8 oz. fresh peas, weighed after shelling
4 oz. macaroni
2 oz. [½ cup] Parmesan cheese, finely grated

In a medium-sized saucepan, bring the water to the boil over high heat. Add the beans and chick-peas and boil them for 2 minutes. Remove the pan from the heat and leave the beans to soak in the pan for 1½ hours.

Replace the pan over high heat and bring the water to the boil. Reduce the heat to low and simmer the beans and chick-peas for 1½ hours, or until they are almost tender. Remove the pan from the heat and drain the beans and peas in a colander. Set aside.

In a large heavy saucepan, fry the salt pork over moderate heat for 5 to 8 minutes, or until it is golden brown all over and has rendered most of its fat. With a slotted spoon, transfer the salt pork to a plate and set aside while you cook the vegetables.

Pour the olive oil into the pork fat and add the onions and garlic to the pan. Fry them, stirring occasionally, for 5 to 7 minutes, or until the onions are soft and translucent but not brown. Add the potatoes, carrots and celery to the pan and continue to cook for a further 5 minutes, stirring constantly. Stir in the cabbage and tomatoes and cook for 5 minutes.

Pour in the chicken stock and add the bouquet garni, chick-peas, beans, salt pork, salt and pepper. Increase the heat to high and bring the soup to the boil. Reduce the heat to low, cover the saucepan and simmer the minestrone for 35 minutes.

Uncover the saucepan and remove and discard the bouquet garni. Add the fresh peas and macaroni and continue to cook the soup for another 10 to 15 minutes, or until the macaroni is 'al dente', or just tender.

Remove the pan from the heat and spoon the soup into serving bowls or into a large, warmed soup tureen. Sprinkle over the Parmesan cheese and serve immediately.

Peasant Soup

A country-style German dish, Peasant Soup may be served either as a first or as a main course. The quantity given in this recipe will be sufficient for 4 people as a main course. Serve this hearty soup with lots of crusty French bread or rolls and butter.

6 SERVINGS

2 oz. [¼ cup] butter
2 lb. stewing steak, cut into small cubes
2 medium-sized onions, roughly chopped
bouquet garni, consisting of 4 parsley sprigs, 1 thyme spray and 1 bay leaf tied together
1 garlic clove, crushed or finely chopped
1 teaspoon paprika
1 teaspoon salt
½ teaspoon freshly ground black pepper
4 tablespoons flour
4½ pints [5½ pints] home-made beef stock
2 large potatoes, peeled and roughly diced
½ tablespoon finely chopped fresh dill or 1 teaspoon dried dill
2 oz. [½ cup] Parmesan cheese, grated

In a large, heavy saucepan, melt the butter over moderate heat. When the foam subsides, add the beef cubes and fry them, turning occasionally, for 5 to 8 minutes or until they are lightly and evenly browned.

Add the onions and fry for 5 to 7 minutes, or until they are soft and translucent but not brown. Add the bouquet garni, garlic, paprika, salt and pepper and stir well.

Mix in the flour, reduce the heat to moderately low and cook, stirring, for 5 minutes. Gradually stir in the stock. Bring to the boil. Cover the pan and simmer for 2 hours, stirring occasionally. Add the potatoes, cover and simmer for a further 45 minutes.

Remove and discard the bouquet garni. Ladle the soup into a large, warmed tureen or individual soup bowls. Sprinkle the top with the dill and grated Parmesan cheese.

Serve very hot.

This meaty soup from Germany is sturdy and nourishing and makes an appetizing, filling meal on its own. Or serve it as a winter first course – but follow it with a light main course!

Pistou
ITALIAN VEGETABLE SOUP

A warming, filling soup made with vegetables and spaghetti, Pistou is given its distinctive flavour by the addition of garlic and basil, pounded together. Serve with crisp bread.

4 SERVINGS

1½ pints [3¾ cups] water
1 teaspoon salt
1 lb. French beans, trimmed, washed and chopped
4 medium-sized potatoes, peeled and cubed
14 oz. canned peeled tomatoes, drained
½ teaspoon freshly ground black pepper
4 oz. spaghetti
2 garlic cloves
3 tablespoons chopped fresh basil or 1½ tablespoons dried basil
2 tablespoons olive oil
2 oz. [½ cup] Parmesan cheese, grated

Fill a large saucepan with the water and add the salt. Place the saucepan over high heat and bring the water to the boil. Add the beans, potatoes, tomatoes and pepper. Reduce the heat to moderately low, cover the pan and cook the vegetables for 20 to 25 minutes or until they are tender.

Uncover the pan and add the spaghetti. Continue to cook for a further 12 to 15 minutes, or until the spaghetti is 'al dente' or just tender.

Meanwhile, place the garlic and basil in a mortar. Pound them together with a pestle until they are well mixed. Add the oil and 2 tablespoons of the soup and continue pounding until the mixture is thoroughly combined.

When the spaghetti is cooked, stir the garlic and basil mixture into the soup.

Remove the pan from the heat. Ladle the soup into individual warmed soup bowls and sprinkle with the Parmesan cheese. Serve at once.

Shrimp Bisque

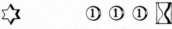

A rich and delicious first course, Shrimp Bisque makes a marvellous start to a meal. Or, serve it with lots of crusty bread and butter for a warming, satisfying lunch.

4 SERVINGS

1 pint [2½ cups] milk
8 fl. oz. double cream [1 cup heavy cream]
8 oz. cooked shrimps, shelled and chopped

12 oz. canned condensed mushroom soup
¼ teaspoon Tabasco sauce
2 tablespoons dry sherry
1 tablespoon chopped fresh dill or 1½ teaspoons dried dill

In a large saucepan, scald the milk over moderate heat (bring just to below boiling point). Remove the pan from the heat and stir in the cream, shrimps, mushroom soup and Tabasco sauce, stirring with a wooden spoon until all the ingredients are well blended.

Return the pan to low heat and gently warm the soup until it is hot but not boiling. Remove the pan from the heat and stir in the sherry.

Transfer the soup to a warmed tureen or individual serving bowls and sprinkle on the dill.

Serve at once.

Tapioca Soup

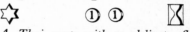

A Thai soup with a delicate flavour, Tapioca Soup should be served very hot and accompanied by bowls of finely chopped spring onions [scallions], finely chopped fresh coriander leaves and diced cucumber.

6-8 SERVINGS

2 pints [5 cups] home-made chicken stock
8 oz. finely minced [ground] pork
½ teaspoon salt
¼ teaspoon freshly ground black pepper
4 oz. [⅔ cup] tapioca
8 oz. crabmeat, fresh or canned, with the shell and cartilage removed
1 small Chinese cabbage, coarse outer leaves removed, washed and shredded
1 tablespoon soy sauce

In a large saucepan, bring the chicken stock to the boil over moderate heat. Add the pork, salt and pepper to the pan, a little at a time, stirring constantly to prevent the meat from sticking together. When all the pork has been added, reduce the heat to moderately low and stir in the tapioca. Simmer the soup, stirring from time to time, for 20 minutes, or until the pork is cooked.

Flake the crabmeat with a fork and stir it into the soup. Add the cabbage. Cover the pan and simmer for a further 2 to 4 minutes, or until the crabmeat is heated through.

Stir in the soy sauce and serve the soup at once.

Vichyssoise

COLD CREAM OF LEEK AND POTATO SOUP

☆   ① ①   ✕ ✕ ✕

A classic cold soup, Vichyssoise, in spite of its French name, is supposed to have been invented in the United States. Whether it is from the New World or the Old, this soup is simply delicious. If you prefer more traditional garnishes, the soup may be sprinkled with chopped chives or parsley rather than the curry powder suggested here.

6 SERVINGS

4 oz. [½ cup] butter
2 lb. leeks, washed, trimmed and chopped
1 lb. potatoes, peeled and roughly chopped

Leeks and cream are the main components of this delicious and elegant version of the classic Vichyssoise.

2 celery stalks trimmed and chopped
1 pint [2½ cups] home-made chicken stock
1 pint [2½ cups] milk
1 teaspoon salt
½ teaspoon freshly ground black pepper
½ teaspoon sugar
¼ teaspoon grated nutmeg
10 fl. oz. double cream [1¼ cups heavy cream]
¼ teaspoon curry powder

In a large saucepan, melt the butter over moderate heat. When the foam subsides, add the leeks, potatoes and celery and fry, stirring constantly, for 8 minutes. Pour in the stock and milk and bring the mixture to the boil. Season the mixture with the salt, black pepper, sugar and nutmeg. Reduce the heat to moderately low, cover the pan and simmer the mixture, stirring occasionally, for 30 to 40 minutes or until the vegetables are soft and cooked through.

Remove the pan from the heat and pour the mixture through a fine strainer into a large mixing bowl. Using the back of a wooden spoon, rub the vegetables through the strainer until only a dry pulp remains. Discard the contents of the

strainer. Alternatively, purée the ingredients in an electric blender.

Stir half of the cream into the purée and set aside to cool. Place the bowl in the refrigerator to chill for at least 4 hours before serving.

To serve, remove the bowl from the refrigerator. Spoon the soup into a large, chilled soup tureen or individual soup bowls and pour a little of the remaining cream into each bowl.

Sprinkle a little curry powder over the soup and serve immediately.

Wonton Soup

 ①

Wonton literally means 'swallowing a cloud' in Chinese, and wontons floating in a clear soup do look rather like clouds billowing in the sky. This delicious soup makes a meal in itself, served with crispy Chinese noodles. You can obtain wonton dough or wrappers from Chinese delicatessens.

6 SERVINGS

1 lb. lean pork or beef, minced [ground]

Wonton Soup is one of the mainstays of Chinese cuisine and you can see why when you sample this delicate yet filling version.

2 tablespoons soy sauce
1-inch piece fresh root ginger, peeled and very finely chopped
1 teaspoon salt
1 teaspoon grated nutmeg
10 oz. frozen chopped spinach, thawed and drained
8 oz. wonton dough, thinly rolled and cut into 36 x 3-inch squares, or 36 bought wonton wrappers
3 pints [7½ cups] home-made chicken stock
1 bunch watercress, washed, shaken dry and very finely chopped

Place the pork or beef, soy sauce, ginger, salt, nutmeg and spinach in a large bowl. Using your fingers, knead well until they are thoroughly blended.

Place the wonton wrappers on a flat working surface. Place a teaspoon of the filling just below the centre of each

wrapper. Using a pastry brush dipped in water, wet the edges of the dough. Fold one corner of the dough over the filling to make a triangle and pinch the edges together to seal. Pull the corners at the base of the triangle together and pinch them to seal. As each wonton is ready, place it on a plate.

Repeat until all the wontons are filled and sealed.

Half-fill a large saucepan with water and place it over high heat. Bring the water to the boil and drop in the wontons. Bring the water to the boil again, reduce the heat to moderate and cook for 5 minutes or until the wontons are tender but still firm.

Remove the pan from the heat. Remove the wontons from the pan and pour off the water. Return the wontons to the pan and pour in the stock. Place the pan over high heat and bring the stock to the boil. Add the watercress. Allow the liquid to come to the boil again. Remove the pan from the heat.

Ladle the soup and wontons into a large, warmed soup tureen or warmed individual soup bowls and serve them at once.

Bread and Cheese Soup

☆ ① ✕

This super soup consists of layers of fried bread and Fontina cheese in beef stock. It is very filling, takes little time to prepare and may be served as a first course or on its own as a luncheon.

4-6 SERVINGS

3 oz. [⅜ cup] butter
12 slices French bread
12 slices Fontina cheese
3 pints [7½ cups] boiling beef stock

In a large frying-pan, melt the butter over moderate heat. When the foam subsides, add the bread slices and fry them for 3 or 4 minutes on each side or until they are crisp and golden. Remove the pan from the heat and transfer the bread to kitchen paper towels to drain.

Preheat the oven to moderate 350°F (Gas Mark 4, 180°C).

Lay the bread slices on the bottom of an ovenproof soup tureen or individual ovenproof serving bowls and top with the cheese slices.

Pour the boiling stock over the bread and cheese and place the tureen or serving bowls in the oven for 10 minutes or until the cheese has nearly melted.

Remove the tureen or serving bowls from the oven and serve at once.

Garbure

SAUSAGE AND CABBAGE SOUP

☆ ① ① ✕ ✕

Garbure is a classic meat and vegetable soup from the Basque country of France. Our adaptation is a somewhat simplified version of the original but loses none of its fine flavour. Served with lots of crusty bread and a tossed salad, it makes a sustaining main meal.

6-8 SERVINGS

1 ham bone
1 teaspoon dried thyme
½ teaspoon salt
¼ teaspoon hot chilli powder
1 large bay leaf
2 pints [5 cups] chicken stock
1 pint [2½ cups] beef stock
1 medium-sized green cabbage, coarse outer leaves removed, washed and coarsely shredded
2 large onions, sliced
3 large carrots, scraped and sliced
12 oz. French beans, washed, trimmed and sliced
8 oz. frozen petits pois
3 large potatoes, thickly sliced
1 celery stalk, cut into ½-inch slices
1 lb. French garlic sausage, skinned and thickly sliced

croûtons, made from day-old white or French bread
1 tablespoon chopped fresh parsley

Place the ham bone, thyme, salt, chilli powder and bay leaf in a large saucepan. Pour in the chicken and beef stock. Stir well and place the pan over high heat. Bring the stock mixture to the boil, stirring constantly.

Add the cabbage, onions, carrots, beans, peas, potatoes and celery. Bring the soup back to the boil. Reduce the heat to low, cover the pan and simmer, stirring occasionally, for 1 hour.

Remove and discard the ham bone and bay leaf. Add the sausage slices and simmer the mixture for 20 minutes.

Remove the pan from the heat and pour the soup into a large warmed soup tureen. Float the croûtons on top, sprinkle on the parsley and serve immediately.

Mussel Chowder

☆ ① ✕

An adaptation of the traditional New England Clam Chowder, Mussel Chowder makes a delicious and rich meal. Serve with warm crusty bread and butter. If fresh mussels are unobtainable, 1 pound of canned and drained mussels may be substituted, omitting the mussel cooking liquid.

4-6 SERVINGS

3 oz. salt pork, diced
2 oz. [¼ cup] butter
2 medium-sized onions, finely chopped
3 potatoes, peeled and chopped
16 fl. oz. [2 cups] chicken stock
2 quarts mussels, scrubbed, steamed, removed from their shells and 5 fl. oz. [⅝ cup] of the cooking liquid reserved
½ teaspoon salt
¼ teaspoon black pepper
¼ teaspoon cayenne pepper
10 fl. oz. double cream [1¼ cups heavy cream]
1 tablespoon chopped fresh parsley

In a large saucepan, fry the salt pork over moderate heat for 5 to 8 minutes or until there is a film of fat covering the bottom of the pan and the cubes resemble small croûtons. With a slotted spoon, transfer the salt pork to kitchen paper towels to drain. Set aside and keep warm.

Add the butter to the pan. When the foam subsides, add the onions and potatoes and cook, stirring occasionally, for 5 to 7 minutes or until the onions are soft and translucent but not brown. Pour over the chicken stock and bring to the boil, stirring occasionally.

Garbure is a classic soup from the Basque country of France and is excellent for informal parties.

Reduce the heat to low, cover the pan and simmer for 5 minutes or until the potatoes are tender but still firm.

Add the mussels with their cooking liquid, the salt, pepper, cayenne and reserved salt pork, stirring to mix well. Increase the heat to high and bring the chowder to the boil. Remove the pan from the heat and gradually stir in the cream.

Pour the chowder into a heated soup tureen, sprinkle over the parsley and serve at once.

Tomato Consommé

☆ ☆ ① ① ✕ ✕

Although this consommé is generally served cold and jellied, it is equally delicious hot.

4 SERVINGS

2 egg whites
1 lb. tomatoes, chopped
2 oz. canned pimientos
2 pints [5 cups] strong cold clarified chicken bouillon
3 fl. oz. [⅜ cup] dry sherry
strip of lemon rind
4 celery stalks, finely chopped

In a small bowl, beat the egg whites with a wire whisk until they are frothy.

Put the tomatoes, pimientos and bouillon into a large saucepan. Whisk in the egg whites, the sherry, the lemon rind and the celery. Place the pan over moderate heat and bring to the boil, whisking constantly. When the mixture comes to the boil, stop whisking and let the boiling liquid rise in the pan. Remove the pan from the heat.

Reduce the heat to very low, return the pan to the heat and simmer gently for 45 minutes.

Let the consommé stand for 15 minutes. Lift off the egg white crust and place it in a strainer lined with cheese-cloth. Pour the consommé through the lined strainer into a large bowl.

Serve hot or cold.

Tomato and Courgette [Zucchini] Soup

☆ ① ✕

Delicious Tomato and Courgette [Zucchini] Soup is a meal in itself, served with crusty bread.

6 SERVINGS

2 lb. ripe tomatoes, blanched, peeled and chopped

6 courgettes [zucchini], trimmed,
  blanched and chopped
3 pints [7½ cups] chicken stock
2 oz. [¼ cup] butter
1 oz. [¼ cup] flour
1 teaspoon salt
1 teaspoon freshly ground black
  pepper
1 teaspoon grated nutmeg
2 teaspoons sugar
1 tablespoon chopped fresh parsley
1 tablespoon chopped fresh dill
4 fl. oz. [½ cup] sour cream

Place the tomatoes, courgettes [zucchini] and half the chicken stock in a large saucepan. Set the pan over high heat and bring the liquid to the boil, stirring frequently. Reduce the heat to moderately low and simmer for 15 to 20 minutes or until the vegetables are soft.

In a small saucepan, melt the butter over moderate heat. Remove the pan from the heat and, with a wooden spoon, stir in the flour to make a smooth paste. Stir in 4 tablespoons of the soup liquid and stir until the mixture is well blended.

Pour the mixture back into the saucepan containing the soup. Cook, stirring constantly, for 2 to 3 minutes or until the soup is smooth and has thickened. Gradually add the remaining stock, stirring constantly, and bring the mixture to the boil. Add the salt, pepper, nutmeg, sugar, parsley and dill, stirring constantly. Remove the pan from the heat and pour the soup into a large, warmed tureen or individual soup bowls.

Stir in the sour cream and serve the soup at once.

Beef

Beef Stew with Corn and Tomatoes

☆ ① ① ① ⋈ ⋈

This hearty winter stew is best if served straight from the casserole, accompanied by a mixed salad.

4 SERVINGS

4 tablespoons paprika
2 lb. topside [top round] of beef, cut into 2-inch cubes
2 oz. [¼ cup] butter
2 medium-sized onions, chopped
2 garlic cloves, crushed
8 oz. canned tomatoes
1 teaspoon dried thyme
1 bay leaf
1 teaspoon salt
½ teaspoon black pepper
2 carrots, scraped and cut into ½-inch rounds
8 fl. oz. [1 cup] dry white wine
1 lb. canned drained sweetcorn
5 fl. oz. single cream [⅝ light cream]
6 tablespoons brandy
2 tablespoons flour

Sprinkle the paprika on a large plate. Roll the beef cubes in the paprika so that they are well coated. Set aside.

In a flameproof casserole, melt the butter over moderate heat. When the foam subsides, add the onions and garlic, reduce the heat to very low and cook for 4 minutes. Add the meat cubes to the casserole, a few at a time, and brown them well. Mix in the tomatoes, thyme, bay leaf, salt, pepper and carrots. Cover the casserole and simmer the stew for 25 minutes.

Pour in the wine, mixing well with a large spoon. Simmer the stew, covered, for another 45 minutes. Add the sweetcorn to the casserole, re-cover and cook the stew for a further 20 minutes.

In a medium-sized mixing bowl, beat the cream, brandy and flour together with a wire whisk. Add the mixture to the stew, stirring to blend thoroughly. Simmer for 15 minutes and serve.

Boeuf Bourguignonne
BEEF AND RED WINE STEW WITH ONIONS AND MUSHROOMS

☆ ① ① ① ⋈ ⋈

Possibly THE classic French country stew, Boeuf Bourguignonne makes a perfect main dish for a special dinner party. Serve with potatoes, green vegetables and a mixed salad, and accompany it with a hearty Burgundy wine.

6-8 SERVINGS

1 tablespoon cooking oil
4 oz. salt pork, cubed

3 lb. topside [top round] of beef, cut into 2-inch cubes
1 carrot, scraped and sliced
1 onion, thinly sliced
1 garlic clove, crushed
1 teaspoon salt
½ teaspoon black pepper
bouquet garni, consisting of 4 parsley sprigs, 1 thyme spray and and 1 bay leaf tied together
½ teaspoon dried thyme
2 tablespoons finely chopped fresh parsley
1¼ pints [3⅛ cups] red wine
1 tablespoon tomato purée
ONIONS
2 oz. [¼ cup] butter
15 small pickling (pearl) onions
½ teaspoon salt
½ teaspoon black pepper
MUSHROOMS
2 oz. [¼ cup] butter
1 lb. button mushrooms, wiped clean and quartered
½ teaspoon grated nutmeg

In a large flameproof casserole, heat the oil over moderate heat. Add the salt pork cubes and fry, stirring occasionally, for 5 to 8 minutes or until they resemble small croûtons and have rendered their fat. With a slotted spoon, transfer them to kitchen paper towels to drain.

Add the beef cubes, a few at a time, and fry them, stirring occasionally, for 5 to 8 minutes or until they are lightly and evenly browned. With a slotted spoon, remove the cubes from the casserole as they brown and set aside.

Add the carrot, onion and garlic to the casserole and fry, stirring occasionally, for 5 to 7 minutes or until the onion is soft and translucent but not brown. Stir in the salt, pepper, bouquet garni, thyme and parsley.

Return the beef cubes and salt pork cubes to the casserole and pour over the wine. Stir in the tomato purée. Bring the liquid to the boil, reduce the heat to very low, cover the casserole tightly and simmer the stew for 1½ hours.

Shortly before the end of the cooking time prepare the onions. In a medium-sized frying-pan, melt the butter over moderate heat. When the foam subsides, add the onions, salt and pepper and fry, stirring occasionally, for 8 to 10 minutes or until the onions are golden brown. With a slotted spoon, transfer the onions to the casserole.

Now prepare the mushrooms. Add the butter to the frying-pan and melt over moderate heat. When the foam subsides, add the mushrooms and nutmeg and fry, stirring occasionally, for 3 minutes or until they are just tender. Using the slotted spoon, transfer the mushrooms to the casserole.

Re-cover the casserole and simmer for a further 15 minutes or until the onions are tender but still firm and the meat is very tender.

Remove the casserole from the heat and serve at once.

Carbonnades à la Flamande
FLEMISH BEEF STEW WITH BEER

☆ ① ① ⋈ ⋈

A beef stew made with beer, Carbonnades à la Flamande is one of Belgium's classic dishes. Serve with buttered noodles and plenty of ice-cold beer.

4 SERVINGS

2 oz. [½ cup] flour
1 teaspoon salt
¼ teaspoon black pepper
2 lb. chuck steak, cut into 1-inch cubes
4 tablespoons vegetable oil
6 medium-sized onions, thinly sliced
2 garlic cloves, crushed
18 fl. oz. [2¼ cups] beer
1 tablespoon soft brown sugar
bouquet garni, consisting of 4 parsley sprigs, 1 thyme spray and 1 bay leaf tied together

Sift the flour, salt and pepper into a small mixing bowl. Roll the cubes of meat in the seasoned flour until they are well coated.

In a flameproof casserole, heat the oil over moderate heat. When the oil is hot, add the meat cubes, a few at a time, and brown them on all sides. As they brown remove them with a slotted spoon and set them aside on a plate.

When all the meat cubes have been browned, add the onions and garlic to the pan and fry them for 8 to 10 minutes or until the onions are soft and translucent but not brown. Add more oil if necessary. Return the meat to the casserole and add the beer, sugar and bouquet garni.

Cover the casserole, reduce the heat to low and simmer the stew gently for about 2¼ to 2½ hours, or until the meat is very tender. After about 2 hours cooking, remove the lid and simmer the stew uncovered for the remaining cooking time. (This will reduce the liquid slightly.) Remove the casserole from the heat, remove and discard the bouquet garni and serve.

Boeuf Bourguignonne – one of the glories of French cuisine.

Daube de Boeuf

FRENCH BEEF STEW

☆ ① ① ✕ ✕ ✕

This classic and surprisingly simple Daube de Boeuf makes an ideal main dish for an informal dinner party. Accompany it with noodles, a green salad and a hearty red vin ordinaire.

6 SERVINGS

3 lb. lean stewing steak, cut into 2-inch cubes
8 oz. streaky bacon, cut into 1-inch strips
4 oz. [1 cup] flour
6 oz. mushrooms, wiped clean and sliced
2 lb. tomatoes, blanched, peeled, seeded and roughly chopped
6 fl. oz. [¾ cup] beef stock

MARINADE

10 fl. oz. [1¼ cups] red wine
2 fl. oz. [¼ cup] brandy
2 tablespoons olive oil
2 teaspoons salt
6 black peppercorns
½ teaspoon dried thyme
1 bay leaf
2 garlic cloves, crushed
4 onions, thinly sliced
4 carrots, scraped and sliced

In a large bowl, combine all the marinade ingredients together and stir well to mix. Add the beef and baste it thoroughly. Cover the dish and place it in the refrigerator. Marinate the beef overnight or for at least 12 hours, basting occasionally.

Half fill a medium-sized saucepan with water and bring it to the boil over moderate heat. Reduce the heat to low, add the bacon and simmer it for 10 minutes. Drain the bacon and pat it dry with kitchen paper towels.

Remove the beef from the marinade and dry it on kitchen paper towels. Strain the marinade into a bowl, reserving both the liquid and the vegetables. Remove and discard the bay leaf.

Preheat the oven to moderate 350°F (Gas Mark 4, 180°C).

Put the flour into a medium-sized bowl. Dip the beef cubes into the flour so that they are well coated on all sides. Shake the cubes to remove any excess flour.

Arrange 2 or 3 strips of the bacon on the bottom of a large flameproof casserole. Spoon a few of the marinade vegetables, mushrooms and tomatoes over the top.

Arrange a layer of beef over the vegetables. Continue making layers of bacon, vegetables and beef, ending with a layer of bacon. Pour the stock and the reserved marinating liquid over the mixture.

Place the casserole over moderate heat and bring the liquid to the boil. Transfer the casserole to the oven and braise for 3½ to 4 hours, or until the meat is very tender.

Remove the casserole from the oven and skim any grease from the surface. Taste and add more salt and pepper if necessary. Serve immediately.

Hungarian Beef Goulasch

A variation of traditional goulasch, this sauce is flavoured with wine. Serve with noodles.

4 SERVINGS

2 lb. chuck steak
4 tablespoons vegetable oil
3 large onions, chopped
2 garlic cloves, crushed
1½ tablespoons paprika
1 tablespoon flour
2 tablespoons tomato puree
1 pint [2½ cups] red wine
    bouquet garni, consisting of 4
    parsley sprigs, 1 thyme spray and
    1 bay leaf tied together
1 teaspoon salt
1 teaspoon black pepper
½ teaspoon dried marjoram
1 red pepper, white pith removed
    and seeded
3 large tomatoes
5 fl. oz. [⅝ cup] sour cream

Trim any excess fat from the meat and cut it into 1-inch cubes. Dry the cubes on kitchen paper towels.

In a large, flameproof casserole, heat the oil over moderate heat. When the oil is hot add the meat cubes, a few at a time, and brown them all over. With a slotted spoon, remove the meat cubes from the casserole as they brown and set them aside.

When all the meat has been browned, reduce the heat to low, add the onions and garlic to the casserole and fry for 5 minutes, stirring occasionally. Add the paprika and stir until the onions are well coated. Stir in the flour, tomato purée and wine. Continue stirring until the liquid comes to the boil.

Return the meat to the casserole with

This colourful Hungarian Beef Goulasch makes a marvellous main course for a festive meal.

the bouquet garni, salt, pepper and marjoram. Cover and simmer over low heat for 2 hours.

While the meat is cooking, cut the red pepper into thin strips. Put the tomatoes in a bowl, cover with boiling water and leave to stand for 1 minute. Pour off the water, peel and chop the tomatoes coarsely.

Add the pepper and tomatoes to the casserole and simmer the mixture for 15 minutes or until the meat is very tender. Remove the bouquet garni and discard it.

Stir in the sour cream, cook for a further 5 minutes and serve.

Umido di Carne
ITALIAN MEAT STEW

Umido di Carne is a very simple but appetizing dish to serve for a festive supper or lunch. Serve with crusty bread.

4-6 SERVINGS

1 oz. [2 tablespoons] butter
2 tablespoons vegetable oil
2 onions, finely chopped
3 garlic cloves, crushed
1 lb. lean beef, cubed
1 lb. lean veal, cubed
3 celery stalks, trimmed and
    finely chopped
2 carrots, scraped and chopped
14 oz. canned peeled tomatoes
1 teaspoon salt
1 teaspoon black pepper
1 teaspoon dried oregano
4 parsley sprigs
1 bay leaf
8 fl. oz. [1 cup] red wine
1 lb. potatoes, peeled and halved

In a large flameproof casserole, melt the butter with the oil over moderate heat. When the foam subsides, add the onions and garlic and fry, stirring occasionally, for 5 to 7 minutes or until the onions are soft and translucent but not brown.

Add the beef and veal to the casserole and fry, stirring frequently, for 6 to 8 minutes or until the meat is browned.

Add the celery, carrots, tomatoes with the can juice, the salt, pepper, oregano, parsley and bay leaf. Pour over the wine. Increase the heat to high and bring the liquid to the boil. Reduce the heat to low, cover the casserole and simmer for 1½ hours. Add the potatoes. Re-cover the casserole and continue cooking for a further 45 minutes or until the meat is very tender when pierced with the point of a sharp knife.

Remove the casserole from the heat. Remove and discard the parsley sprigs and bay leaf. Serve at once.

Ecuadorian Lamb Stew

A tasty and colourful dish, Ecuadorian Lamb Stew should be served in a ring of saffron rice. A well-chilled bottle of light white wine, such as Sylvaner or Riesling would go well with this dish.

4 SERVINGS

3 fl. oz. [⅜ cup] olive oil
1 medium-sized onion, roughly chopped
2 garlic cloves, crushed
14 oz. canned peeled tomatoes, drained and chopped
1 red pepper, white pith removed, seeded and thinly sliced
1 green pepper, white pith removed seeded and thinly sliced
½ teaspoon hot chilli powder
1 teaspoon coriander seeds, coarsely crushed
1 teaspoon salt
2 lb. boned leg of lamb, cubed
8 fl. oz. [1 cup] dry white wine
2 tablespoons chopped fresh coriander leaves

In a medium-sized saucepan, heat half the oil over moderate heat. Add the onion and garlic and fry them for 5 to 7 minutes, or until the onion is soft and translucent but not brown. Add the tomatoes, red and green peppers, chilli powder, coriander seeds and salt and stir to mix. Reduce the heat to low, cover the pan and simmer for 15 minutes.

In a large frying-pan, heat the remaining oil over moderate heat. When the oil is hot, add the lamb cubes a few at a time and fry them for 6 to 8 minutes, or until they are browned all over. As the meat browns, remove it from the pan with a slotted spoon and transfer it to the pan with the vegetables. Stir in the wine and fresh coriander leaves. Cook, covered, for 50 minutes to 1 hour or until the meat is tender.

Remove from the heat and serve the stew immediately.

Serve exotic Ecuadorian Lamb Stew with saffron-flavoured rice for a really different dish.

Greek Lamb Stew

Delicious and easy-to-make, Greek Lamb Stew makes a warming main dish. Serve with lots of flat Greek bread, a tossed mixed salad and some light red wine, such as Demestica.

6 SERVINGS

4 fl. oz. [½ cup] olive oil
2½ lb. lean lamb, cut into 2-inch cubes
2 lb. small new potatoes, scrubbed and halved
8 oz. small pickling (pearl) onions, peeled
14 oz. canned peeled tomatoes, drained and chopped
5 oz. tomato purée
6 fl. oz. [¾ cup] red wine
2 tablespoons wine or malt vinegar
2 teaspoons salt
3 bay leaves
1 tablespoon lemon juice
3 oz. [½ cup] blanched almonds
6 oz. feta cheese

Greek Lamb Stew is a super mixture of lamb, potatoes, onions, wine and cheese. Serve with lots of pita (flat Greek bread) and red wine.

In a large, deep frying-pan, heat the olive oil over moderate heat. When the oil is hot, add the meat to the pan and, stirring and turning occasionally, cook for 5 minutes, or until the meat is lightly browned on all sides. With a slotted spoon remove the meat from the pan and set it aside.

Add the potatoes and onions to the pan and, stirring and turning occasionally, cook the vegetables for 8 minutes, or until the onions are lightly browned.

Meanwhile, in a small saucepan bring the tomatoes, tomato purée, red wine, vinegar and salt to the boil, stirring frequently. Remove the pan from the heat and set the tomato sauce aside.

When the onions are browned, return the meat to the frying-pan and stir in the tomato sauce. Add the bay leaves. Reduce the heat to low, cover and simmer the stew, stirring occasionally, for 1 to 1¼ hours, or until the lamb is tender when pierced with the point of a sharp knife.

Stir in the lemon juice and blanched almonds and crumble the cheese on top of the stew. Cook the mixture for a further 5 to 8 minutes, or until the cheese has melted.

Remove the pan from the heat and transfer the stew to a warmed serving dish. Serve at once.

Navarin Printanier
MUTTON STEW WITH FRESH SPRING VEGETABLES

☆　①　✕ ✕

A traditional French country dish, Navarin Printanier is the perfect dish for a dinner party. It is traditionally made with fresh young spring vegetables, but frozen vegetables may be substituted if necessary. Serve with a tomato salad and lots of light red wine, such as Brouilly.

6 SERVINGS

4 oz. salt pork, diced
1½ lb. boned breast of mutton, trimmed of excess fat and cut into 2-inch cubes
1½ lb. boned shoulder of mutton, trimmed of excess fat and cut into 2-inch cubes
2 tablespoons soft brown sugar
1 teaspoon salt
½ teaspoon freshly ground black pepper
½ tablespoon flour

6 medium-sized tomatoes, blanched peeled, seeded and chopped
2 pints [5 cups] chicken stock bouquet garni, consisting of 4 parsley sprigs, 1 thyme spray and 1 bay leaf tied together
2 oz. [¼ cup] butter
12 small potatoes, peeled
6 small turnips, peeled
6 small carrots, scraped
12 small pickling (pearl) onions, peeled
½ tablespoon white sugar

In a large, heavy-bottomed saucepan, fry the salt pork over moderate heat for 5 to 8 minutes, or until it resembles small croûtons and has rendered most of its fat. Stir occasionally to prevent it from sticking to the bottom of the pan. With a slotted spoon, transfer the salt pork to a large plate.

Add the meat cubes, a few at a time, to the pan and fry, stirring and turning occasionally, for 6 to 8 minutes, or until all of the cubes are lightly and evenly browned.

With a slotted spoon, transfer the meat to the plate with the salt pork. Keep warm while you brown the remaining meat cubes in the same way.

Remove the pan from the heat and pour off half of the fat. Return the meat cubes and salt pork to the pan and sprinkle over the brown sugar, salt and pepper. Place the pan over moderate heat and cook, stirring constantly with a

wooden spoon, for 3 minutes, or until the sugar has caramelized. Add the flour to the pan and cook for a further 3 minutes, stirring constantly with the wooden spoon.

Stir in the tomatoes, chicken stock and bouquet garni. Increase the heat to moderately high and bring the liquid to the boil. Reduce the heat to low, cover and simmer for 1 hour.

Meanwhile, prepare the vegetables. In a large frying-pan, melt the butter over moderate heat. When the foam subsides, add the potatoes, turnips, carrots and onions and cook, stirring occasionally, for 8 to 10 minutes or until the onions are golden brown. Stir in the white sugar and cook for a further 3 minutes or until the sugar has dissolved. Remove the pan from the heat. With a slotted spoon, transfer all of the vegetables to a dish and keep warm.

Remove the saucepan from the heat. With a metal spoon, skim off any scum from the surface of the cooking liquid. Add the browned vegetables and stir well. Return the pan to the heat and cook for 25 minutes, or until the meat and vegetables are tender when pierced with the point of a sharp knife.

Remove the pan from the heat. With a metal spoon, skim off any scum from the surface of the cooking liquid. Remove and discard the bouquet garni. Transfer the stew to a warmed, deep serving dish or individual serving plates.

Serve immediately.

Saute d'Agneau

LAMB SAUTE

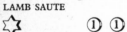

A sophisticated meat dish, Sauté d'Agneau is simple to prepare and cook. To make the dish slightly richer, espagnole or demi-glace sauce may be used instead of the stock suggested here, although this will increase the length of preparation time. Serve with petits pois and sautéed potatoes.

4 SERVINGS

3 tablespoons olive oil
2 lb. boned shoulder of lamb, trimmed of excess fat and cut into ½-inch cubes
1 celery stalk, trimmed and chopped
1 medium-sized onion, finely chopped
4 fl. oz. [½ cup] red wine
8 fl. oz. [1 cup] beef stock
1 tablespoon cornflour [cornstarch], mixed to a paste with 2 tablespoons water
2 tablespoons tomato purée
½ teaspoon salt
½ teaspoon freshly ground black pepper
1 teaspoon finely grated lemon rind
4 oz. button mushrooms, wiped clean and thinly sliced

In a large flameproof casserole, heat 2 tablespoons of the olive oil over moderately high heat. When the oil is hot, add the lamb cubes and fry them, stirring frequently, for 10 to 12 minutes or until they are well browned all over. Using a slotted spoon, transfer the meat to a plate and keep warm.

Reduce the heat to moderate and add the remaining tablespoon of oil to the

Smooth and creamy, Sauté d'Agneau is the perfect main dish for that mid-week dinner party – it's quick and easy to make and inexpensive, too.

casserole. Add the celery and onion and fry them, stirring occasionally, for 5 to 7 minutes or until the onion is soft and translucent but not brown. Pour the wine and stock into the casserole, stir in the cornflour [cornstarch] mixture and bring the liquid to the boil, stirring constantly. Return the meat to the pan and add the tomato purée, salt, pepper, lemon rind and mushrooms. Cover the casserole and cook the mixture for 20 minutes, stirring occasionally. (If you prefer your meat well done, increase this final cooking time by 10 minutes.)

Remove the casserole from the heat and serve immediately.

Pork Balls in Wine Sauce

Serve this tasty dish with buttered rice, spinach and a lightly chilled rosé wine.

4 SERVINGS

1½ lb. minced [ground] pork
8 oz. lean bacon or gammon, minced [ground]
4 oz. [2 cups] fresh breadcrumbs
1 large egg
1 teaspoon salt
½ teaspoon black pepper
½ teaspoon ground allspice
2 tablespoons chopped fresh parsley
8 fl. oz. [1 cup] dry sherry
8 fl. oz. [1 cup] chicken stock
2 tablespoons wine vinegar
1 tablespoon sugar
1 teaspoon salt
4 teaspoons cornflour [cornstarch] dissolved in 3 tablespoons water

Preheat the oven to moderate 350°F (Gas Mark 4, 180°C).

In a large mixing bowl, combine the pork, bacon or gammon, breadcrumbs, egg, salt, pepper, allspice and parsley. Using your hands, mix and knead the ingredients until they are well combined.

Shape the mixture into 12 balls. Place the balls, in one layer, in a large baking dish.

In a small saucepan, combine the sherry, stock, vinegar, sugar and salt over low heat, stirring constantly. When the sugar has dissolved, bring the mixture to the boil. Reduce the heat to low and stir in the cornflour [cornstarch] mixture. Cook, stirring constantly, until the sauce has thickened slightly.

Remove the pan from the heat and pour the sauce over the meatballs. Put the meatballs in the oven and bake them for 1½ hours, basting occasionally.

Remove the baking dish from the oven and serve immediately, from the dish.

Pork Goulasch

Serve this delicious stew with buttered noodles, tomato salad and a well-chilled Hungarian Riesling.

4 SERVINGS

2 oz. [¼ cup] butter
2 lb. pork fillets, cubed
3 onions, thinly sliced
2 garlic cloves, crushed
1½ lb. canned sauerkraut, drained
½ teaspoon dried dill
1 teaspoon caraway seeds
1 teaspoon salt
1 teaspoon black pepper
8 fl. oz. [1 cup] chicken stock
8 fl. oz. [1 cup] sour cream

In a large, flameproof casserole, melt the butter over moderate heat. When the foam subsides, add the pork cubes, a few at a time, and cook them, turning occasionally, for 6 to 8 minutes or until they are lightly and evenly browned. Transfer the cubes, as they brown, to a plate.

Add the onions and garlic to the casserole and cook, stirring occasionally, for 5 to 7 minutes or until the onions are soft and translucent but not brown. Stir in the sauerkraut, dill, caraway seeds, salt, pepper and stock and bring to the boil.

Return the pork cubes to the casserole and stir well to mix. Reduce the heat to low, cover the casserole and simmer the goulasch for 1 to 1¼ hours or until the pork is very tender.

Stir in the sour cream and serve at once.

Tasty Pork Balls in Wine Sauce.

Pork and Pineapple Casserole

☆ ☆   ① ① ①   ⧖ ⧖

This delicately-flavoured dish of pork fillets cooked with herbs, pineapple, orange, wine and green peppers makes a superb Sunday lunch. Serve with creamed potatoes and buttered green beans.

4 SERVINGS

4 pork fillets, beaten until thin
1 garlic clove, halved
1 teaspoon salt
½ teaspoon black pepper
1 tablespoon grated orange rind
½ teaspoon dried marjoram
½ teaspoon dried sage
1 oz. [2 tablespoons] butter
2 medium-sized green peppers, white pith removed, seeded and cut into julienne strips
10 fl. oz. [1¼ cups] dry white wine
16 oz. canned pineapple rings, drained and coarsely chopped
1 tablespoon cornflour [cornstarch] dissolved in 2 tablespoons orange juice

Rub the pork fillets all over with the garlic clove halves and half of the salt and pepper. Discard the garlic clove halves and lay the pork fillets flat on a working surface. Sprinkle over the orange rind, marjoram and sage. Roll up the fillets and secure the rolls with trussing thread or string. Set aside.

In a medium-sized flameproof casserole, melt the butter over moderate heat. When the foam subsides, add the green peppers and fry them, stirring frequently, for 4 minutes. With a slotted spoon, remove the peppers from the casserole and set them aside.

Add the pork fillets to the casserole and fry for 6 to 8 minutes, turning the rolls occasionally with tongs, or until they are lightly browned.

Pour the wine into the casserole and stir in the remaining salt and pepper, the pineapple pieces and fried green peppers. Bring the liquid to the boil, stirring constantly. Reduce the heat to low, cover the casserole and simmer for 50 minutes to 1 hour, or until the pork fillets are cooked and tender when pierced with the point of a sharp knife.

Remove the casserole from the heat. Using a slotted spoon, remove the pork rolls from the casserole and transfer them to a warmed serving dish. Remove and discard the trussing thread or string.

Tender pork fillet rolls cooked with pineapple chunks, green pepper and white wine, Pork and Pineapple Casserole tastes as superb as it looks.

Remove the pineapple pieces and green peppers from the casserole and arrange them around the meat. Keep the mixture warm.

With a metal spoon, skim off and discard any fat from the surface of the cooking liquid in the casserole. Pour the liquid through a fine wire strainer into a medium-sized saucepan and stir in the cornflour [cornstarch] mixture. Set the pan over moderate heat and cook the sauce, stirring constantly with a wooden spoon, for 5 minutes or until it is thick and smooth.

Remove the pan from the heat. Pour the sauce over the pork rolls and serve immediately.

Pork Ratatouille

☆   ① ① ①   ⧖ ⧖

This adaptation of a Belgian recipe may be served with mashed potatoes or fried rice for a superb lunch or supper.

4 SERVINGS

2 lb. pork fillets, cut into 2-inch cubes
2 teaspoons salt
1 teaspoon black pepper
2 fl. oz. [¼ cup] olive oil
1 large onion, finely chopped
2 garlic cloves, crushed
1 large red pepper, white pith removed, seeded and chopped
1 large green pepper, white pith removed, seeded and chopped
3 large courgettes [zucchini], trimmed and sliced
1 small aubergine [eggplant], chopped and dégorged
14 oz. canned peeled tomatoes
4 fl. oz. [½ cup] dry white wine
2 teaspoons grated lemon rind
14 oz. canned white haricot beans, drained

Rub the pork cubes with the salt and pepper and set aside.

In a large flameproof casserole, heat the oil over moderate heat. When the oil is hot, add the onion, garlic, peppers, courgettes [zucchini], aubergine [eggplant] and tomatoes with the can juice. Fry, stirring and turning occasionally, for 8 to 10 minutes or until the onion is soft. Add the pork, pour over the white wine and stir in the lemon rind. Bring the liquid to the boil.

Reduce the heat to low and simmer the mixture for 1 hour. Add the haricot beans and simmer for a further 20 minutes or until the pork is very tender when pierced with the point of a sharp knife.

Remove the casserole from the heat and serve at once.

Pork Vindaloo

☆   ① ①   ⧖ ⧖

A pungent, strongly flavoured curry from the west coast of India, Pork Vindaloo is for those who like really hot curries. If you do not have an electric blender, use ground spices.

4-6 SERVINGS

2-inch piece fresh root ginger, peeled and chopped
4 garlic cloves, chopped
1½ teaspoons hot chilli powder
2 teaspoons turmeric
1 teaspoon salt
seeds of 6 whole cardamom
6 cloves
6 peppercorns
1 x 2-inch cinnamon stick
2 tablespoons coriander seeds
1 tablespoon cumin seeds
5 fl. oz. [⅝ cup] wine vinegar
2 lb. pork fillets, cut into large cubes
4 curry leaves (optional)
3 tablespoons vegetable oil
1 teaspoon mustard seeds
5 fl. oz. [⅝ cup] water

Put the ginger, garlic, chilli powder, turmeric, salt, cardamom seeds, cloves, peppercorns, cinnamon stick, coriander seeds, cumin seeds and the vinegar into an electric blender. Blend the mixture at high speed for 30 seconds. Scrape down the sides of the blender and blend for another 30 seconds. Add more vinegar if necessary and blend until the mixture forms a smooth liquid paste.

Place the pork in a large mixing bowl and mix in the spice paste. Cover the bowl and set it aside to marinate for 1 hour at room temperature. Lay the curry leaves, if you are using them, on top. Re-cover the bowl and place it in the refrigerator for 24 hours, turning the meat 2 or 3 times during that time.

Two hours before cooking time, remove the bowl from the refrigerator and set aside at room temperature.

In a large saucepan, heat the oil over moderate heat. When the oil is hot, add the mustard seeds. Cover the pan to stop the seeds from spattering and, when they stop popping, add the pork, all the marinade and the water. Stir to mix and bring the mixture to the boil. When the curry boils, reduce the heat to low, cover the pan and simmer for 40 minutes. Uncover the pan and continue cooking for a further 40 minutes or until the pork is very tender and the sauce is neither too thick nor too thin.

Remove the pan from the heat. Spoon the vindaloo into a large warmed serving dish. Serve immediately.

Blanquette de Veau

☆ ☆ ① ① ⊠ ⊠

*Served with boiled rice and garnished with
sautéed mushrooms, Blanquette de Veau is
an ideal main dish to serve for a dinner
party.*

4 SERVINGS

1½ lb. lean boned veal, cut into
   1½-inch cubes
2 medium-sized onions, studded
   with 2 cloves each
2 carrots, scraped and quartered
3 fl. oz. [⅜ cup] white wine
   bouquet garni, consisting of 4
   parsley sprigs, 1 thyme spray and
   1 bay leaf tied together
½ teaspoon salt
⅛ teaspoon white pepper
1½ oz. [3 tablespoons] butter
6 tablespoons flour
5 fl. oz. single cream [⅝ cup light cream]
2 egg yolks
8 toast triangles

Put the veal cubes in a large saucepan and
pour in enough water to cover. Bring the
water to the boil over moderate heat and
cook the veal for 2 minutes.

Skim off any scum from the top of the
liquid and reduce the heat to low. Add
the onions, carrots, wine, bouquet garni,
salt and pepper. Cover the saucepan and
simmer over low heat for 1½ hours, or

*Lean veal chunks in a rich cream
sauce, Blanquette de Veau is a classic
French dish which makes an excellent centrepiece for a special dinner.*

until the meat is tender when pierced
with the point of a sharp knife.

Strain off the liquid into a bowl and
reserve 1¼ pints [3⅛ cups] for the sauce.
Keep warm while you make the sauce.

In a saucepan, melt the butter over low
heat. Remove the pan from the heat and
stir in the flour with a wooden spoon.
Stirring constantly, gradually add the
reserved stock. Return the pan to the
heat and cook, stirring constantly, for 2
to 3 minutes or until the sauce becomes
thick and smooth. Remove the sauce
from the heat.

In a small bowl, beat the cream and
egg yolks together with a wooden spoon.
Stir 4 tablespoons of the hot sauce, a
spoonful at a time, into the cream-and-
egg yolk mixture. When the sauce is well
mixed with the cream and egg yolks,
return it to the saucepan gradually, beating it with a wire whisk. Replace the
saucepan on low heat and cook, stirring,
until the sauce just boils.

Transfer the veal to a heated serving
dish and pour the sauce over it.

Garnish with the toast triangles and
serve immediately.

Osso Buco

STEWED VEAL KNUCKLE OR SHANK

☆ ① ① ⊠ ⊠

*One of the internationally recognized
classics of Italian cuisine, Osso Buco is
made from veal knuckle or shank with a
sauce of tomatoes and wine. Osso Buco is
traditionally served with risotto milanese.*

6 SERVINGS

3 oz. [¾ cup] seasoned flour, made
   with 3 oz. [¾ cup] flour, 1 teaspoon
   salt and ½ teaspoon black pepper
3 lb. veal knuckle or shank, sawn
   into 3-inch pieces
4 oz. [½ cup] butter
1 large onion, thinly sliced
14 oz. canned peeled tomatoes
2 tablespoons tomato purée
6 fl. oz. [¾ cup] dry white wine
1 teaspoon salt
½ teaspoon black pepper
1 teaspoon sugar
GREMOLADA
1 tablespoon grated lemon rind
2 garlic cloves, crushed
1½ tablespoons chopped fresh
   parsley

Place the flour on a plate and dip in the
veal pieces, one by one, to coat them.
Shake off any excess. Set aside.

In a large, flameproof casserole, melt
the butter over moderate heat. When

the foam subsides, add the veal pieces and cook, turning occasionally, for 5 to 8 minutes or until they are evenly browned. Transfer the veal to a plate. Set aside.

Add the onion to the casserole and cook, stirring occasionally, for 5 to 7 minutes or until it is soft and translucent but not brown. Add the tomatoes with the can juice and the tomato purée and cook, stirring occasionally, for 3 minutes. Add the wine, salt, pepper and sugar. Bring the mixture to the boil.

Return the veal pieces to the casserole and stir well. Reduce the heat to low, cover the casserole and simmer the veal for 1½ to 2 hours or until it is very tender.

Meanwhile make the gremolada. In a small mixing bowl, combine the lemon rind, garlic and parsley.

Stir the gremolada into the veal mixture. Cook for a further 1 minute. Remove the casserole from the heat and transfer the veal pieces to a warmed serving dish. Spoon over the sauce and serve at once.

Veal Marengo

☆ ① ① ① ⧓ ⧓

This classic French stew may be served with puréed potatoes, French beans and a well-chilled strong white wine such as Meursault.

6 SERVINGS

3 lb. lean boned veal, cubed
2 teaspoons salt
2 teaspoons black pepper
3 oz. [⅜ cup] butter
2 fl. oz. [¼ cup] vegetable oil
2 onions, thinly sliced
2 garlic cloves, crushed
4 fl. oz. [½ cup] dry white wine
4 fl. oz. [½ cup] veal or chicken stock
  bouquet garni, consisting of 4
  parsley sprigs, 1 thyme spray and
  1 bay leaf tied together
8 oz. canned tomatoes, chopped
2½ oz. tomato purée
1 teaspoon paprika
12 small pickling (pearl) onions,
  peeled
12 oz. button mushrooms, wiped
  clean and sliced
1 tablespoon flour

Place the veal cubes on a working surface and sprinkle over 1 teaspoon of salt and 1 teaspoon of pepper. Set aside.

In a large flameproof casserole, melt 2 ounces [¼ cup] of the butter with the oil over moderate heat. When the foam subsides, add the onions and garlic and cook, stirring occasionally, for 5 to 7 minutes or until the onions are soft and translucent but not brown. Stir in the veal cubes and cook them, turning from

time to time, for 8 to 10 minutes or until they are evenly browned.

Pour in the wine and stock and stir in the bouquet garni, the tomatoes with the can juice, the tomato purée and paprika. Bring the liquid to the boil, stirring occasionally. Reduce the heat to low, cover the casserole and simmer the mixture for 1½ hours. Add the pickling (pearl) onions and simmer for a further 30 minutes or until the meat is very tender.

Meanwhile, in a large frying-pan, melt the remaining butter over moderate heat. When the foam subsides, add the mushrooms and cook, stirring frequently, for 3 minutes. Remove the pan from the heat and, with a slotted spoon, transfer the mushrooms to a deep, warmed serving dish. When the veal is cooked, using a slotted spoon, add the veal cubes and pickling (pearl) onions to the serving dish. Set the mixture aside.

Remove the casserole from the heat and strain the contents into a saucepan, pressing the vegetables and flavourings with the back of a wooden spoon to extract all the juices. Place the pan over moderately high heat, bring the liquid to the boil and boil for 10 minutes or until the liquid has reduced by about one-third. Stir in the flour, a little at a time, and cook, stirring constantly, for 2 to 3 minutes or until the sauce has thickened slightly.

Remove the pan from the heat and pour the sauce over the meat and vegetable mixture. Serve at once.

Veal and Rice Casserole

☆ ① ① ⧓ ⧓

This delicious Austrian casserole is quick and easy to prepare. Serve it with a green salad.

4 SERVINGS

2 oz. [¼ cup] butter
4 tablespoons vegetable oil
2 lb. boned veal shoulder, cubed
2 onions, finely chopped
2 tablespoons paprika
1 pint [2½ cups] chicken stock
2 fl. oz. [¼ cup] white wine
1 teaspoon salt
½ teaspoon black pepper
1 teaspoon dried thyme
10 oz. [1⅜ cups] long-grain rice,
  washed, soaked in cold water for
  30 minutes and drained

In a large flameproof casserole, melt the butter with the oil over moderate heat. When the foam subsides, add the meat and onions and fry, stirring frequently, for 5 to 8 minutes or until they are brown.

Stir in the paprika. Add the stock, wine, salt, pepper and thyme. Bring to the boil. Reduce the heat to low, cover the casserole and simmer for 1¼ hours.

Stir in the rice, re-cover the casserole and simmer for a further 20 to 25 minutes, or until the rice is tender and has absorbed all the liquid. Serve at once.

Veal and Rice Casserole.

Coq au Vin
CHICKEN COOKED IN RED WINE

☆ ① ① ① ⊠ ⊠

One of the great classics of French cuisine, Coq au Vin makes an ideal dish for a dinner party. Serve with boiled new potatoes and steamed broccoli.

4 SERVINGS

  3 oz. [⅜ cup] butter
  4 slices bacon, finely chopped
  1 x 4 lb. chicken, cut into serving
    pieces
  1 teaspoon salt
  1 teaspoon black pepper
  2 fl. oz. [¼ cup] brandy, warmed
  1¼ pints [3⅛ cups] red wine
  10 fl. oz. [1¼ cups] chicken stock
  1 tablespoon tomato purée
  1 garlic clove, crushed
    bouquet garni, consisting of 4
    parsley sprigs, 1 thyme spray and
    1 bay leaf tied together
  16 small onions, peeled
  8 oz. mushrooms, wiped clean and
    sliced
  1 oz. [2 tablespoons] butter blended
    to a paste with 1 oz. [4 tablespoons]
    flour
  2 tablespoons finely chopped fresh
    parsley

Preheat the oven to moderate 350°F (Gas Mark 4, 180°C).

In a large flameproof casserole, melt 1 ounce [2 tablespoons] of butter over moderate heat. When the foam subsides, add the bacon and fry, stirring occasionally, for 5 to 8 minutes or until it is crisp. With a slotted spoon, remove the bacon to a plate.

Add the chicken pieces and fry, stirring and turning occasionally, for 8 to 10 minutes or until they are lightly but evenly browned. Stir in the salt and black pepper. Carefully pour over the brandy and ignite, shaking the casserole gently until the flames die away.

Return the bacon to the casserole and pour over the wine and stock; add the tomato purée, garlic and bouquet garni. Stir well to mix and bring the liquid to the boil.

Cover the casserole and place it in the oven. Braise the chicken for 40 minutes.

Meanwhile, prepare the onions and mushrooms. In large frying-pan, melt 1 ounce [2 tablespoons] of butter over moderate heat. When the foam subsides, add the onions and cook, stirring and turning occasionally, for 8 to 10 minutes or until they are golden brown. Reduce the heat to low and simmer the onions, stirring occasionally, for a further 15 minutes or until they are just tender.

In a second frying-pan, melt the re-

Chicken cooked slowly in red wine – that's succulent Coq au Vin, a classic French country dish.

maining butter over moderate heat. When the foam subsides, add the mushrooms and fry, stirring occasionally, for 3 minutes or until they are just tender.

Remove the casserole from the oven and add the onions and mushrooms to the mixture. Return the casserole to the oven and continue to braise the chicken for a further 15 to 20 minutes or until it is tender.

Remove the casserole from the oven and, using a slotted spoon, transfer the chicken, onions and mushrooms to a warmed plate. Cover and keep warm while you finish off the sauce.

Place the casserole over high heat and bring the liquid to the boil. Boil the liquid until it has reduced to about 1 pint [2½ cups]. Using a slotted spoon, skim any scum from the surface of the liquid and remove and discard the bouquet garni. Stir in the butter and flour mixture, a little at a time, and cook the sauce, stirring constantly, for 2 minutes or until it is smooth and has thickened.

Return the chicken, onions and mushrooms to the casserole and stir well to blend. Simmer for 2 minutes, then remove the casserole from the heat. Sprinkle over the parsley and serve at once.

Venison Stew

☆ ① ① ⊠ ⊠ ⊠

Serve Venison Stew with a tossed green salad, crusty bread and some red wine for a really special meal.

4 SERVINGS

2 lb. lean venison, cut into 2-inch cubes
2 oz. [¼ cup] butter
1 teaspoon salt
½ teaspoon freshly ground black pepper
1 teaspoon dried rosemary
3 medium-sized carrots, scraped and quartered
1 small turnip, peeled and roughly chopped
8 oz. small onions, peeled
3 medium-sized potatoes, peeled and halved
14 oz. canned peeled tomatoes
3 tablespoons tomato purée
MARINADE
12 fl. oz. [1½ cups] red wine
8 fl. oz. [1 cup] beef stock
3 tablespoons olive oil
1 large onion, thinly sliced
8 black peppercorns
3 garlic cloves, crushed
2 tablespoons chopped fresh parsley
1 teaspoon dried rosemary
bouquet garni, consisting of 4 parsley sprigs, 1 thyme spray and 1 bay leaf tied together

In a large, shallow dish, combine all the marinade ingredients. Add the venison cubes and mix well. Set aside and marinate the meat at room temperature for at least 12 hours, basting it from time to time.

Remove the meat from the marinade and dry it on kitchen paper towels. Reserve the marinade.

In a large flameproof casserole, melt the butter over moderate heat. When the foam subsides, add the meat cubes and cook, stirring and turning occasionally, for 8 minutes, or until the cubes are lightly and evenly browned. Add the reserved marinade, the salt, pepper and rosemary and stir well. Bring the liquid to the boil, skimming off any scum that rises to the surface. Reduce the heat to low, cover and simmer the stew for 1½ hours.

Add the carrots, turnip, onions, potatoes, tomatoes with the can juice and the tomato purée and stir thoroughly to blend.

Re-cover the casserole and continue to simmer the stew for a further 1 hour, or until the meat is tender when pierced with the point of a sharp knife.

Remove the casserole from the heat and remove and discard the bouquet garni. Serve at once.

Lean venison chunks marinated overnight then cooked with vegetables, Venison Stew makes a really hearty sustaining main course for a winter meal.

Couscous

☆ ☆   ① ①   ◰ ◰ ◰

Serve Couscous with a green salad. If you do not have a couscoussier, you can construct a temporary one by placing a cheesecloth-lined colander on top of a saucepan, sealing the space between the colander and the rim of the pan with a twisted, damp tea towel.

6 SERVINGS

5 tablespoons vegetable oil
3 garlic cloves, crushed
4 green chillis, finely chopped
3 lb. boned leg of lamb, cubed
2 teaspoons salt
¾ teaspoon black pepper
1 teaspoon cayenne pepper
2 teaspoons ground cumin
2 teaspoons paprika
1 lb. couscous
18 fl. oz. [2¼ cups] lukewarm salted water
4 oz. [⅔ cup] raisins
2 oz. [¼ cup] chick-peas, soaked overnight and drained
½ teaspoon saffron threads soaked in 1 teaspoon water
3 teaspoons turmeric
2 teaspoons ground coriander
4 tablespoons melted butter

In the lower part of a *couscoussier*, heat 4 tablespoons of the vegetable oil over moderate heat. Add the garlic and chillis and cook, stirring occasionally, for 3 minutes. Add the meat, salt, pepper, cayenne, cumin and paprika to the *couscoussier* and stir to mix well. Pour in 2 pints [5 cups] of water. Bring the water to the boil over high heat, reduce the heat to low and simmer the mixture, covered, for 1 hour.

Meanwhile, put the couscous grains into a large mixing bowl. Pour over 16 fluid ounces [2 cups] of the lukewarm salted water. Leave the couscous to soak for 1 hour, or until it swells slightly. Drain the grains and set them aside.

Pour a further 1 pint [2½ cups] water into the *couscoussier*, increase the heat to high and bring the liquid to the boil. Reduce the heat to low and simmer for a further 30 minutes.

Add the raisins, chick-peas, saffron, turmeric and coriander to the *couscoussier* and mix well. Pour the couscous grains into the steamer or top part of the *couscoussier* and fit it on to the lower part. Steam the couscous, covered, for 40 minutes.

Remove the top part from the *couscoussier* and set it aside. Transfer the couscous grains to a large mixing bowl and pour on the melted butter, the remaining 2 fluid ounces [¼ cup] of lukewarm salted

water and 1 tablespoon vegetable oil. Leave the mixture for 15 minutes. Stir the couscous, breaking up any lumps that have formed, and return the grains to the steamer. Fit the steamer on top of the *couscoussier* again. Steam over low heat, covered, for a further 20 minutes. Remove the *couscoussier* from the heat and serve.

Danish Chicken Casserole

☆   ①   ◰ ◰

A tempting and easy-to-make dish, Danish Chicken Casserole is ideal to serve for lunch or supper.

6 SERVINGS

2 oz. [½ cup] flour
1 teaspoon salt
½ teaspoon black pepper
2 teaspoons dried dill
1 x 5 lb. chicken, skinned and cut into 8 serving pieces
2 eggs, lightly beaten
2 oz. [¼ cup] butter
2 tablespoons vegetable oil
10 fl. oz. [1¼ cups] chicken stock
1 medium-sized green pepper, white pith removed, seeded and cut into thin rings
2 tomatoes, blanched, peeled and sliced
4 fl. oz. double cream [½ cup heavy cream]
2 oz. [½ cup] Samsoe or Cheddar cheese, grated

In a plate or bowl, combine the flour, salt, pepper and dill together. Dip the chicken pieces in the beaten eggs and then in the flour mixture.

In a large flameproof casserole, melt the butter and oil over moderate heat. When the foam subsides, add the chicken pieces to the pan and fry them for about 8 minutes, or until they are lightly browned on all sides, turning frequently with tongs or large spoons.

Add the chicken stock to the pan and bring the liquid to the boil. Reduce the heat to low, cover the pan and simmer the chicken gently for 50 minutes, or until it is tender.

With a slotted spoon, remove the chicken pieces from the pan and arrange them in the centre of a warmed, large flameproof serving dish. Keep the chicken warm while you are finishing the sauce.

Preheat the grill [broiler] to moderate.

Add the green pepper to the liquid in the frying-pan and simmer for 4 minutes. Add the tomatoes and cook for a further 2 minutes.

With a slotted spoon, remove the vegetables from the liquid and arrange them around the chicken pieces. Remove

the pan from the heat and stir the cream into the liquid. Return the pan to the heat and cook gently for 2 to 3 minutes.

Pour the sauce over the chicken. Sprinkle the cheese on top and place the dish under the grill [broiler] for 5 minutes or until the cheese is bubbling.

Serve immediately.

Pork Curry

☆   ① ①   ◰ ◰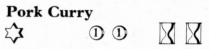

This is a spicy, pungent curry which is best served with plain boiled rice and an onion and tomato salad.

6 SERVINGS

1 tablespoon ground coriander
1 teaspoon ground cumin
1 teaspoon hot chilli powder
1½ teaspoons turmeric
½ teaspoon ground cinnamon
½ teaspoon ground cardamom
½ teaspoon ground cloves
½ teaspoon black pepper
3 tablespoons vinegar
4 tablespoons vegetable oil
3 onions, finely chopped
3 garlic cloves, crushed
2-inch piece fresh root ginger, peeled and finely chopped
2 to 3 green chillis, finely chopped
3 lb. pork fillets, cubed
1½ teaspoons salt
1 teaspoon sugar
1½-inch slice creamed coconut dissolved in 1 pint [2½ cups] boiling water

In a small mixing bowl, combine the coriander, cumin, chilli powder, turmeric, cinnamon, cardamom, cloves and black pepper. Pour over the vinegar and stir until the mixture forms a smooth paste.

In a large saucepan, heat the oil over moderate heat. When the oil is hot, add the onions and fry, stirring occasionally, for 8 to 10 minutes or until they are golden brown.

Add the garlic, ginger and chillis and fry, stirring frequently, for 3 minutes. Add the spice paste and fry, stirring constantly, for 10 minutes. If the mixture gets too dry add a spoonful of vinegar or water. Add the pork cubes and fry, stirring frequently, for 6 to 8 minutes or until the pork no longer looks raw. Add the salt and sugar and pour over the coconut mixture. Stir the mixture and bring it to the boil. Cover the pan, reduce the heat to low and simmer the curry for 1 to 1¼ hours or until the pork is very tender. Serve immediately.

Couscous is ideal for entertaining.

Rabbit Stew

☆   ① ①   ⧖ ⧖ ⧖

This delicious country stew is an excellent supper party dish. Accompany it with a full-bodied Burgundy wine, such as Nuits St. Georges, or a well-chilled white wine, such as Vouvray.

4 SERVINGS

- 1 x 4 lb. rabbit, cleaned and cut into serving pieces
- 2 oz. [¼ cup] butter
- ½ teaspoon salt
- ½ teaspoon white pepper
- ½ teaspoon dried thyme
- ½ teaspoon dried rosemary
- 1 tablespoon prepared French mustard
- 1 tablespoon cornflour [cornstarch] dissolved in 2 tablespoons single [light] cream
- 4 fl. oz. [½ cup] port
- 3 oz. [½ cup] sultanas or seedless raisins
- 3 oz. [½ cup] currants

MARINADE
- 16 fl. oz. [2 cups] dry white wine
- 4 fl. oz. [½ cup] olive oil
- 10 oz. dried prunes
- 2 garlic cloves, crushed
- 1 teaspoon salt
- ½ teaspoon freshly ground black pepper
- 1 medium-sized onion, thinly sliced
- 1 carrot, scraped and thinly sliced

GARNISH
- 1 tablespoon chopped fresh parsley
- 6 crescent-shaped croûtons

First prepare the marinade. Place all the marinade ingredients in a large, shallow bowl and stir well to blend. Add the rabbit pieces and marinate them at room temperature, basting occasionally, for at least 6 hours.

Remove the rabbit pieces from the marinade and pat them dry with kitchen paper towels. Reserve the marinade.

In a large, deep frying-pan, melt the butter over moderate heat. When the foam subsides, add the rabbit pieces to the pan and fry them, turning occasionally with tongs, for 8 to 10 minutes or until they are lightly and evenly browned.

Add the marinade to the pan and bring the liquid to the boil, stirring occasionally. Stir in the salt and pepper. Reduce the heat to low, cover the pan and simmer the rabbit for 1 to 1¼ hours or until it is

This warming, satisfying Rabbit Stew takes quite a long time to prepare and cook, but the end result is well worth the effort. Serve with red wine for a special dinner.

very tender when pierced with the point of a sharp knife.

Remove the pan from the heat and transfer the rabbit pieces to a heated serving dish. Keep warm while you prepare the sauce.

Strain the cooking liquids into a medium-sized saucepan and, using tongs, remove the cooked prunes and add them to the saucepan. Discard any pulp left in the strainer. Place the pan over moderate heat and bring the liquid to the boil. Stir in the thyme and rosemary. Reduce the heat to low and add the mustard and the cornflour [cornstarch] mixture, stirring gently. Add the port, sultanas or seedless raisins and currants and simmer gently for 10 minutes.

Pour the sauce over the rabbit in the heated serving dish. Sprinkle with chopped parsley and arrange the croûtons around the sides of the serving dish.

Serve immediately.